MODERN MURDER
Yearbook

The
MODERN MURDER
Yearbook

Edited by
JONATHAN GOODMAN

ROBINSON
LONDON

Robinson Publishing Ltd
7 Kensington Church Court
London W8 4SP

First published by Robinson Publishing Ltd 1994

A copy of the British Library Cataloguing in Publication
Data for this title is available from the British Library

ISBN 1-85487-184-6

Typeset by Hewer Text Composition Services, Edinburgh
Printed in EC

10 9 8 7 6 5 4 3 2 1

Contents

Preface

THIS IS A NEW DEPARTURE for me, in the sense that though I have written or edited rather a lot of books about murders, I have always steered clear of very recent cases – which, though they or picturesque parts of them seem likely to be memorable, may not pass the test of time. There is no single reason why some briefly newsworthy cases take permanent lodgings in the memory or, when looked at years later by people like myself, appear to deserve retelling – or why other cases, also the stuff of front-page stories with banner headlines, lack retrospective interest.

Leaving aside the cases that live on or are revived solely or mainly because of unanswered questions or unsolved riddles, I believe that longevity is less often dependent upon what a case is all about than upon just one or two eccentric details – perhaps to do with the setting of the crime (for instance, the Red Barn at Polstead, Suffolk, in which Maria Marten was killed and buried in 1827; the bell-less belfry of the Emanuel Baptist Church, San Francisco, where the body of Blanche Lamont was found in 1895; the crab-apple tree in the lovers' lane in New Brunswick, New Jersey, which shaded the bodies of the Reverend Edward Hall and his also-married mistress Eleanor Mills in 1922). Or perhaps to do with clothing (for instance, the swell-elegant black satin dress worn by Maria Manning at her trial and her public execution, on both occasions alongside her dowdy husband Fred, in London in 1849; the topper cut down to bowler-height by Franz Müller, who had taken the hat in mistake for his own after committing the very first murder on a British train in 1864; the boy's outfit worn by Dr Crippen's mistress Ethel Le Neve, alias Master Robinson, on the

Canada-bound *s.s. Montrose* in 1910). Or perhaps to do with – no, I shall stop there, for fear that I have already laboured the point.

Most of the accounts in this book are of cases tried or otherwise apparently ended in 1992 or thereabouts. The couple of others, of older cases, are included because the cases have been brought back to public notice by revisionists.

I am grateful to the friends who have contributed essays or items – also, for help in finding or verifying information, to David Allen; Fay Bradley; Nicolas Bragge; Dr Lewis Gavin; Dr Alan Keightley; Esther F. Lardent of the American Bar Association; Ross McCarthy of the *Birmingham Post & Mail*; Kevin E. Tokata, Deputy Prosecuting Attorney for the City and County of Honolulu; Dr Helen Whitwell.

The Reason Why

Even when, in Great Britain, the crime of murder carried the risk of heavier punishments than it does now, some people, clearly or at least legally sane, committed murder for reasons that were either inadequate to the crime or, in the view of most other sane people, very peculiar. But (and I admit that I may be suffering from a sort of optical illusion, my eyes having lighted upon reports of a few cases that my mind has increased to an extraordinary many) it seems that there has recently been a spate of actual or attempted murders with tiny or quaint motives.

Among the reports I have bothered to clip, I find one about a middle-aged homosexual, Robert Bryan, who became so vexed that his youthful partner, Matthew Hay, invariably beat him when they played chess at their flat in south-west London ('I dreaded playing with him because I always, but always, lost') that he obtained a pistol in preparation for their next onesided game and, as soon as Hay smirked 'checkmate', shot him through what he thought was the heart. Apparently his knowledge of anatomy was no better than his ability at chess, and he succeeded only in committing attempted murder, for which he was sentenced to ten years' imprisonment . . .

Twenty-six-year-old Dean Kingston, having become divorced from Tina, the mother of their three children, persuaded her to re-marry him, and four days after the ceremony at Carshalton, when they had a tiff, strangled her – a crime for which, since for some reason it was designated as manslaughter, he was put away for five years . . .

Norman Waller, a thirty-four-year-old resident of

Gateshead, who used a chisel to stab to death one of a number of young men whom he suspected were thinking of stealing his car, was cleared of murder but found guilty of affray . . .

Stuart McNab, a sixteen-year-old Glaswegian, repeatedly stabbed Alan Donegan, who was thirty-three, after failing to cadge a cigarette from him, and then fled to an island in the Hebrides, where police found him under a bed, together with three knives, one of them the murder weapon. Found guilty at the Glasgow High Court, he was ordered to be detained indefinitely . . .

Richard Yates, a thirty-three-year-old convicted sex-offender, living in Swindon, took one of his four daughters, Nicola, aged ten, for a walk in a park, and when she asked him what a rapist was, got angry over the innocent question and throttled her with a jumper. Leaving her lying in a copse, he went to a pub, where he laughed and joked and played darts with friends. The body lay in the copse for two days before it was noticed. At the end of Yates's trial at Bristol Crown Court, during which his counsel explained that 'his daughter touched a raw spot and he simply lost control', he was jailed for life.

Anyone who is not a Roman Catholic (and, I hope it is true to say, most of those who are) will surely be flummoxed by Noeleen Hendley's motive for the murder by proxy of her white-haired husband Anthony – which, to quote the man who did the job for her, 'was because she could not divorce him, as she was such a devout Roman Catholic.'

Mrs Hendley – who, pencil-thin herself, ran slimming clubs in Derby – and Terence McIntosh, a dark but balding widower, the same age as her and her husband, forty-six, met for the first time, and instantly fell head over heels in love, when they got together in July 1991 to plan the wedding of her son to his daughter. She told him, not so tearfully as to smudge her mascara, that her husband was repugnant to her; that she had managed for some time to avoid having sexual intercourse with

2

him by pretending to be 'disabled'. As soon as the of-course-Catholic wedding ceremony was over, McIntosh proposed to her, but was regretfully turned down for the reason you know. Eventually, they began discussing what seemed to them to be the only alternative, and McIntosh mentioned that he knew a man who might be willing, if the price was right, to 'help them out'. After they had decided what price *was* right, McIntosh met the prospective hireling, forty-one-year-old Paul Buxton, in a pub, and persuaded him to accept the . . . er . . . assignment on the basis of a down-payment of £1,000, £1,500 once the task was completed, and subsequent payments totalling £3,000.

Though the short-sighted Buxton turned out to have little aptitude as a contract killer, he was admirably perseverant. Four attempts had to be called off at the last minute: one because a farm labourer put in an appearance when Buxton was getting ready to attack Hendley on his way home across fields from the restaurant where he worked as a chef; another because Buxton, having been let into the Hendleys' semi-detached house by the wife when the husband was ill in bed, was so frightened by a pet cat that he took to his heels, very nearly knocking Mrs Hendley over as he rushed past her to escape.

The fifth attempt was more successful. It was on the night of Sunday, 3 November – which by coincidence was the eve of the Hendleys' silver-wedding anniversary. While McIntosh took Hendley out drinking, Mrs Hendley let Buxton into the house and showed him where to hide (presumably she had taken the precaution of putting the alarming cat out). When Hendley returned and went upstairs, Buxton, wearing a black mask and gloves, rushed across the landing and beat him about the head with a rolling-pin, striking him twenty-nine times. After Mrs Hendley had handed Buxton the £1,500 completion instalment and he had carefully punched her in the face – so that she would have evidence that she, as well as her husband, had been attacked by a burglar – he hurried back to his home in the village of Loscoe, where he burned not only his complete murder-outfit but also his spectacles and wrist-watch before taking a bath.

Though Hendley's skull was, in the words of a detective, 'fractured like an eggshell', he was able to crawl to his bed. His wife having screamed to a neighbour to call the emergency services, he was rushed to a hospital. Two days later, doctors established that he was brain-dead, and the life-support machine was switched off.

The police were taken in by Mrs Hendley's burglar tale. She appeared on television news programmes – looking very fetching in black, weepy-eyed at her sudden widowhood (she was not wearing eye make-up), and wincing every so often at the pain from her single injury – to plead for help in identifying the masked burglar-murderer. She gave interviews to newspapers, saying that the culprit had to be caught; if she had her way, he would be hanged. Meanwhile, she received a payment of £70,000 from a life assurance company.

But then things started to go wrong. Her fault. Prior to the crime, she had let on to an indiscreet friend that she was having an affair, and now a friend of the friend told that to the police, who, identifying the adulterer as McIntosh, obtained a print-out of his phone calls – and discovered that he had phoned Buxton, a bit of a suspicious character, a few hours before the murder.

Buxton, brought in for questioning, soon admitted his involvement in the crime – but insisted that he had not committed murder. He said that the minute he came face-to-face with Hendley, he lost his resolve, and hit him just five or six times, and only with his hand, so as to get past him and out of the house: 'Every time I have shut my eyes since, I have seen *his* eyes. If you want the killer, arrest his wife.'

The police did so. They also arrested McIntosh, who within a short while confessed to his considerable role in the conspiracy. Unlike many criminal confessors, Catholic or not, he stuck to his words, even till his trial at Nottingham Crown Court, when he pleaded guilty.

4

His insistence on the truth was most unhelpful to the barristers who afterwards defended the other two (who, said the oratorical prosecutor, Brian Escott-Cox, QC, 'were consumed with a terrible passion which brooked no interference – once the seeds had been planted, the Devil gave it increase'). The jury returned verdicts of guilty against them as well, and they also were sentenced to life imprisonment. Thereupon, the Widow Hendley fainted on to the floor of the dock – understandably considering that she knew, among other tragic things, that her contribution to the instalments paid to Buxton had been wasted, that the life assurance company would be reclaiming its seventy grand, and that she was unlikely ever again to clap eyes or any other part of her body on the man she had yearned for so religiously.

Usurping the Rainbow

The Kidnapping of Sidney Reso

ALBERT BOROWITZ

As usual, Sidney J. Reso woke early on Wednesday, 29 April 1992. He had breakfast with his wife Patricia, his childhood sweetheart to whom he had been married for thirty-seven years. Performing a tender family ritual, Patricia straightened her husband's tie and adjusted his breast-pocket handkerchief; she had concluded many years ago that, although Sid's warm smile remained as winning as ever, he 'definitely was not a clothes horse'. At 7.30 a.m. Reso kissed his wife goodbye, taking pains as he did at every parting to tell her that he loved her.

The Resos lived in Morris Township, in northern New Jersey, at the end of a wooded cul-de-sac which they shared with only three neighbours. The location was ideal, because it offered both a rural setting and a convenient fifteen-minute drive to Sid Reso's office in Florham Park. At the age of fifty-seven, Reso, a stocky brown-haired man 'whose voice had a trace of a Southern lilt', was a Vice President of the Exxon Corporation which he had served since 1957 in various assignments in the United States, Australia and London; in 1987 he had been appointed President of the Exxon Company International, the division responsible for Exxon's oil and gas operations outside North America. Admired in Exxon as an effective manager completely free of flamboyance or idiosyncracies, Reso did not aspire to become a darling of the business media and was virtually unknown outside the company.

From his youth, he had built his life on the bedrock of two permanent loyalties – to Patricia and the Exxon Corporation. He had spent his entire career with Exxon after receiving his bachelor's degree in petroleum engineering from Louisiana State University in 1957. His initial assignment was to an apparently exhausted oil-field of the Humble Oil Refining Company in the remote town of New Iberia, Louisiana. Murray Hawkins, one of Reso's professors at Louisiana State, recalled how his star pupil turned this first challenge into an eye-catching success:

'The joke around the company was that he was being exiled to New Siberia, because there wasn't much going on there. But when he arrived there, he got busy, looked at all the maps and found a bunch of oil that hadn't been tapped in the wells, about seven million gallons.'

By 1983, Reso's rise to prominence in Exxon's empire had won him a distinguished-alumnus award from his alma mater. The citation noted that 'engineers all over the world look to Sidney J. Reso as an engineer who has reached the pinnacle of success.' Despite his professional distinction and business attainments, Reso refrained from power politics; colleagues regarded him as a career executive who was direct but not abrasive, not a 'desk-pounder'. One oil executive said of him, 'You wouldn't mistake him for a drugstore clerk, but he's not Lee Iacocca.'

Sid Reso's 'workaholic' business schedule and his frequent international trips left him little time for leisure; although he loved golf, he was rarely seen on the links of his country club in Morris Township. The single-minded devotion to Exxon may have exacted a toll on Reso's health, however, because in 1989 he suffered a heart attack and was prescribed a course of medication to guard against a recurrence. An even heavier blow befell Sid and Patricia when they lost one of their five adult children to complications of AIDS. These personal trials

7

had the effect of binding the family even more closely together.

The pattern of the Resos' well-ordered lives broke up abruptly on the morning of 29 April 1992. A little before nine, a neighbour noticed Reso's car standing, with its engine running, at the end of his 250-foot driveway near Jonathan Swift Road. The neighbour called Reso's office and was told that he had not come in. Someone from Exxon promptly telephoned Patricia Reso, who hurried down the driveway to investigate. She found that the car, its doors closed, was still where the neighbour had seen it and that its motor continued to idle. Peering into the car, she immediately made an observation that persuaded her that her husband had not left the scene voluntarily. The decisive clue was that the key was still in the ignition. Never, she reasoned, would her husband, who was 'fanatical' about such matters, have abandoned his key – not even if, as she had first feared, he had suffered another heart attack as he set out for work that morning. In such a crisis and any other extremity imaginable, he would surely have had the presence of mind to keep the key with him. Suspecting, therefore, that he had been kidnapped, Mrs Reso took a tissue paper from her pocket and wrapped her hand so that she would not smudge any fingerprints as she opened the car door and retrieved the key.

In the days following Reso's disappearance, a barrage of messages purporting to originate from his kidnappers were directed to the Exxon Corporation and to the executive's wife. At the insistence of the self-proclaimed abductors, the FBI established a cellular phone to receive their future messages. Despite this compliance on the part of investigators, both federal and state authorities continued to refer to the disappearance as a 'missing person' case, pending receipt of hard evidence that Reso was actually in the hands of captors. On Sunday, 3 May, however, a caller contacted the FBI with instructions regarding a ransom drop. An arrangement was made for a further message to be phoned to a booth in a restaurant parking lot, but the call never came.

On Thursday, 7 May, the New York *Post* reported a bizarre development in the case: a group calling itself 'the Warriors of the Rainbow' had contacted Exxon's offices in Florham Park and claimed to be holding the missing executive. The story led Morris County Prosecutor W. Michael Murphy, Jr, to issue a statement which appeared to confirm the receipt of a ransom demand but expressed scepticism about the involvement of the shadowy group that had been identified in the *Post* article. Mr Murphy said:

'As you know, a New York City daily newspaper has printed unconfirmed allegations regarding communications from a group maintaining that they have Mr Reso in their custody. It would be inappropriate for this office to discuss this report of a communication in the absence of verification that the communication is indeed from an individual or group holding Mr Reso in their custody. Absent a current photograph or voice recording, this office cannot come to the conclusion that Mr Reso is in the custody of any particular group.'

To the press, however, the name of the self-advertised kidnappers suggested the intriguing possibility that Reso had been taken by 'green' terrorists acting in revenge against perceived sins by Exxon against the environment. The *New York Times* reminded its readers that 'the name Rainbow Warrior belonged to a ship owned by the environmentalist group Greenpeace that was sabotaged and sunk in 1988.' Indignant at the usurpation of the name of its tragically lost ship, Greenpeace denied involvement in Reso's disappearance; its executive director, Steve D'Esposito, maintained that 'for 20 years Greenpeace has steadfastly adhered to the principle of nonviolence.'

On Friday night, 15 May, Patricia Reso, elegant and self-possessed, appeared on a New Jersey television station to plead for her husband's return. 'I'm making a personal appeal to some people who I want to believe have my husband with them,' she said. 'I know in my heart that he's alive, and pray that he is healthy. I want you to know that I have received your message. But it is so important to me that my kids and I have assurance that he is alive and unharmed. I am willing to do whatever is necessary to have him reunited with us. I hope that he will be released very soon. I love Sidney and want him to come back home to us. Lastly, I am asking the news media to stop any speculation as to who you may be and what your goals are. I simply want my husband back with the family.'

After the broadcast, the authorities revealed that Mrs Reso had made her plea in accordance with instructions contained in a one-page note that had been taped to a light-pole in the parking lot of the Townsquare Mall in Rockaway Township, New Jersey, earlier in the day. An anonymous call to the mall's security office had led to the discovery of the note.

As the weeks went by with the Reso mystery unsolved, security experts debated the case in the press. A former assistant United States attorney expressed his view that the seizure of Reso was not a terrorist act or one that had a political or corporate target. Otherwise, 'the kidnappers would certainly have created publicity for themselves.' Michael Hershman, president of an international investigating agency, warily observed that the case did not follow any of the norms of kidnapping: 'If you kidnap somebody,' he explained, 'you want to give yourself as much time as possible to get away. You don't leave the guy's car in the driveway for someone to discover, for someone to sound the alarm immediately.'

Despite the voices of these doubters, Mrs Reso maintained her contact with the people she believed were holding her husband. On Tuesday, 16 June, seven weeks after Sid Reso's disappearance, Patricia Reso called a televised news conference in her living-room to renew her plea for the return of her husband. Seated near her fireplace, she read a short statement to make it clear that she and Exxon officials 'unconditionally' wanted Sid Reso back. 'Since the time of his disappearance,' she said, 'Mothers' Day has passed and our family has been greatly troubled. We desperately miss him and eagerly look forward to being reunited with him. It is my hope and prayer that my husband will join us for Fathers' Day this Sunday. Sid, please, if you can hear me, know that we love you, we miss you and we pray for you every day.'

On the day of Mrs Reso's second television appearance, a prerecorded telephone call was received by the investigating authorities, directing them to pick up a ransom letter in a mailbox on Route 24 in Morris Township. The letter ordered that $18.5 million in used $100 bills be placed in laundry bags of a specified type for delivery in accordance with subsequent instructions.

On Thursday evening, 18 June, monitors of the FBI cellular telephone received messages from male and female callers signalling that their demands for delivery of the ransom were at last approaching the 'end game'. Beginning at 9.08 p.m., a series of telephone calls and written messages led the investigators on a four-hour pursuit along a tortuous route through three New Jersey counties surrounding the Reso home. The trail laid by the kidnappers bore a grotesque resemblance to the 'scavenger hunts' that were once a favoured playtime activity in America's camps and suburbs:

9.08 p.m.: In a call from a pay telephone at the train station in Gladstone, the searchers were told to look for an envelope at a designated place in Morristown.

9.33 p.m.: The FBI recovered a note in Morristown, containing instructions to proceed to the Ralston General Store in Mendham, New Jersey, about 5 miles away.

9.50 p.m.: At the Mendham store the FBI picked up a note which directed them to a building on Route 24, near Chester, New Jersey.

11

10.09 p.m.: Arriving at the building near Chester, the FBI found written instructions leading them to a plant in Peapack, New Jersey. There the agents were to await further orders.

10.40 p.m.: A male caller using a pay telephone booth at the Chester Mall gave additional instructions.

11.16 p.m.: A woman was observed near telephones at the Somerset Hills Elks Club in Gladstone, from which three calls had been made to the FBI cellular telephone earlier in the day. The woman was seen walking towards a white Mercedes-Benz.

It was the 10.40 p.m. telephone call from the Chester Mall that proved to be the kidnappers' undoing. A female member of the large FBI surveillance force that saturated northern New Jersey sighted a male suspect using one of the mall's telephone booths. The man appeared to be wearing latex gloves, a strange accoutrement for a mild spring night. The agent saw the man drive away in an Oldsmobile after he had completed his call; she pursued the car until she could make a note of its licence plate, which was then traced to a rental agency in Hackettstown, New Jersey. A good night's work done, the agent was confident of success. 'This is the kidnapper,' she had thought as soon as she distinguished the latex gloves in the light cast by the telephone booth. 'This is the man we've been waiting to find for 50 days.'

At 12.50 on Friday morning, the FBI closed in on the Hackettstown car rental agency, where they confronted a man returning the Oldsmobile. He told them that his name was Arthur D. Seale, Jr, and that he was waiting for his wife to pick him up. Mrs Seale arrived shortly afterwards in a white Mercedes in which investigators found pairs of rubber gloves and a briefcase containing a 1985 directory of home addresses for Exxon executives.

As the FBI agents compared notes on their pursuit of

the kidnappers during the course of the feverish night, the crucial role played by the sharp-eyed surveillance agent in the Chester Mall was thrown into stronger relief. The main force of agents assigned the duty of following the complex ransom instructions had ultimately lost the trail, for the series of calls from the kidnappers had ended abruptly. The apparent reason was that Arthur Seale, driving the Oldsmobile with FBI investigators in close pursuit, had panicked as he approached a roadblock that had been set up because of a fire near Far Hills, New Jersey. Seale had reversed direction suddenly and driven off, not to be seen again until the final rendezvous at the car rental agency.

Overnight, the Seales, both forty-five years old, became New Jersey's most celebrated kidnappers since Bruno Richard Hauptmann, and their biographies were quickly reconstructed. Like his father, Seale had joined the Hillside, New Jersey, police department, where he won many commendations that were offset by repeated warnings for excessively aggressive behaviour. After a motor-vehicle accident, he retired from the force on a disability pension in the late 1970s and was subsequently employed by Exxon as a security officer for ten years, rising to a post that brought him an annual salary of $65,000.

As they entered their middle years, Seale and his wife, Irene Jacqueline (Jackie), who had been a manager of a local winery, decided that only a change in career would bring them their rightful share of the American Dream. Unlike their victim, Sid Reso, who would probably have agreed with the adage of American real-estate magnate Trammell Crow that 'work is more fun than fun,' the Seales equated happiness with life among the rich and leisured. In late 1987 the Seales bade New Jersey goodbye and moved to Hilton Head Island, South Carolina, where they bought an outdoor furniture and interior decoration business near the entrance to the Palmetto Dunes resort. Friends said that Mrs Seale entered the venture with some experience in retail

13

business. Her family, the Szarcos, had once operated a liquor store and delicatessen in Hillside, New Jersey, and the young Jackie had grown up in comforts that she longed to rediscover and grandly surpass. The couple purchased a home well beyond their means in the Sea Pines Plantation, a resort community on the fashionable southern end of Hilton Head, and amassed hundreds of thousands of dollars in debt. After the furniture business failed, the Seales, with their two teenage children Justin and Courtney, pulled up stakes in the middle of the night. Their next destination on the pleasure map of America was the ski resort of Vail, Colorado, where Arthur Seale reincarnated himself as a securities broker. By late 1989 this new venture had also proved a failure and the Seales, now bankrupt, returned to New Jersey, where they took up temporary residence with Arthur's retired parents, at their home in Changewater, a hamlet on the Musconetcong River in the western part of the state. As they cast their minds over the disappointments they had suffered during the past few years, Arthur and Jackie could not bring themselves to surrender their dreams of affluence. In fact, as recently as several days before his arrest, Arthur Seale had paid a visit to their son Justin in Hilton Head and nostalgically reminisced with acquaintances about their lives there in the 1980s, telling a dinner companion that he was considering returning to buy a marina.

Shortly after they were taken into custody, the Seales were charged in New Jersey state court with kidnapping, extortion and conspiracy and were subsequently indicted by a federal grand jury in Newark on related charges. At first the couple remained silent, but Jackie Seale was the first to crack, bargaining her cooperation for leniency in sentencing. Guided by information from Jackie, investigators, in a twelve-hour search on Saturday, 27 June, recovered the decomposing body of Sidney Reso from a three-foot-deep grave in the Pine Barrens, a desolate stretch of sandy woods near Atlantic City.

Jackie detailed the tortures to which she and her

husband had subjected Reso before his death. They had constructed as his prison a coffin-like wooden box, 6 feet 4 inches long, $3^1/2$ feet wide and 3 feet high; the lid was punctured with airholes and padlocked on three sides. When they had kidnapped Reso in his driveway, Arthur Seale had shot the executive in the arm in the course of a scuffle; they had handcuffed him, placed duct-tape on his eyes and mouth, and laid him on his back in their hand-made wooden box, trussed to a pile of blankets so as to restrain his movements. They had then driven to a storage facility in western New Jersey where they had rented an unventilated metal compartment. It was here that they had stowed their victim until he died on Sunday, 3 May, after four days of their barbarous treatment.

Prior to Reso's death, Jackie told authorities, they had visited their victim several times a day, giving him water but no food; in her considered opinion, Reso had died of 'natural causes'. The police firmly rejected her diagnosis, although the autopsy could not pinpoint the cause of death; asphyxiation, dehydration, and complications from the gunshot-wound were all implicated as likely contributing factors. Even a younger man, who had never suffered a heart attack, would have had difficulty surviving four days in the Seales' stifling torture chamber.

As soon as the Seales found their captive dead on the Sunday morning, Jackie told her questioners, they had buried his body in the Pine Barrens. The death of Reso, far from deterring them from chasing their dream of extorting millions of dollars, had spurred them to accelerate their plans immediately. It was on the Sunday evening that they had contacted the authorities to initiate their first instructions for delivery of the ransom; according to Jackie, their failure to fix a rendezvous on that occasion was due to her error in scrambling the numbers of the parking-lot telephone where the FBI agents were awaiting the kidnappers' message.

Faced with his wife's defection, Arthur Seale also confessed to federal and state authorities. In November 1992 he was sentenced to ninety-five years in federal prison and fined $1 3/4 million so as to capture any money he might receive from books or movies about the crime; later he was sentenced to an additional forty-five years in the New Jersey prosecution. In January 1993 Jackie Seale was sentenced by the federal court to twenty years in prison for her part in the kidnapping. Judge Garrett E. Brown, Jr, rejected her argument that she was a battered wife who had been forced into crime by her husband, but took cognizance of her cooperation with law enforcement officials. Pursuant to the plea bargain that was struck for her assistance to the investigation, the State of New Jersey also imposed a twenty-year sentence on Mrs Seale, to run concurrently with her federal sentence.

In an interview with Barbara Walters in Passaic County Jail that was broadcast on the ABC-TV programme '20/20' on 13 November 1992, Arthur Seale, weeping when he liked, maintained that he had always been a 'hardworking, moral, decent individual' and that he and his wife 'really epitomized most of the American ethic.' They were two 'normal people driven to absolute desperation' by the sense that all avenues of life had been closed to them. Although they had been living with Seale's parents since the Vail bankruptcy, they had been ordered to leave the house by the end of the school-year. Seale said that he was particularly concerned about his daughter Courtney, who had run away from home in Colorado and suffered from bulimia in addition to a frenzy of self-mutilation, in which she had cut off her hair and stuck pins in her skin; he attributed her troubled state to the fact that at the age of eleven she had been raped by three men on a beach in the Seales' Hilton Head paradise.

As Arthur and Jackie reviewed their plight, the idea of kidnapping, inspired by their memories of the successful ransom of an Exxon executive who had been captured and returned unharmed in South America some years before, had commended itself as a 'one-time reward' that would not have to involve their hurting their victim. From the directory of Exxon executives' addresses, they had chosen Reso as their victim because of his secluded residence. Arthur Seale had planned that, after they collected the $18½ million that they would demand, he and Jackie could once again live a 'middle-class life,' reserving only a modest amount of the plunder for themselves while 'giving bags of money away to "fun" charities.'

During his conversation with Barbara Walters, Seale insisted that his love for Jackie remained undiminished even after she had led the police to the body and blamed him for having compelled her participation in the crime. In a particularly mawkish moment of the interview, Arthur appropriated as his own sentiments the opening lines of Elizabeth Barrett Browning's 'How Do I Love Thee'. Despite his sudden lyricism, he lost no opportunity to emphasize the active part his wife had played in planning and carrying out the kidnapping.

The couple had initially conceived the idea of hiding their victim in a self-haul trailer, but none was small enough to fit into the metal storage facility they intended to lease as Reso's prison. This difficulty had inspired them to build a wooden box – which Seale asserted was much more like a 'closet' than a 'coffin'. Jackie had helped him build the box and drill the airholes and had taken turns with him in trying out the interior to assure themselves that Reso's body would comfortably fit inside.

It was Jackie, Seale told Walters, who had employed an ingenious ruse designed to lure Reso out of his car where he could be overpowered with less of a struggle. When they had arrived in the Resos' neighbourhood on the morning of 29 April, the trim Jackie had jogged by their target's home in her running outfit and moved the Resos' morning newspaper from one side of the driveway to the other, intending that Sid would have to leave his car to retrieve the paper. Seale claimed that this strategem had worked to perfection: as Reso emerged from his automobile, the kidnappers' rented van with Jackie at the wheel had blocked the driveway, and Arthur, gun in hand, had confronted their victim. In the television interview, Seale was careful to inform Barbara Walters that his wife was similarly armed. At the time of the kidnapping, Seale was dressed in jeans, a dark sweater and a ski-mask to induce Reso to take him for a terrorist. Ordering Reso to get into the van, Arthur had fastened a handcuff to his victim's right wrist, and as he moved to attach the other handcuff, Reso had suddenly moved, causing Seale's gun to discharge. The bullet had hit Reso's left forearm, and although the wound, Seale asserted, was superficial, the accident was so unexpected as to throw the kidnappers into a temporary panic. Still, they had pushed the injured man into the van and Jackie had sped away, stopping for gauze at a drugstore to treat the wound; Barbara Walters was left to wonder which of the efficiently collaborating pair had provided the duct-tape for their victim's eyes and mouth.

Although acknowledging the justice of Walters' assertion at the beginning of the ABC broadcast that some members of the public might regard him as a monster, Seale claimed in his defence that he and Jackie had visited their victim three times a day and allowed him to exercise by walking on the spot inside the wooden box. He expressed surprise at his wife's earlier statement to police that Reso was given only water. Despite her contrary recollection, he was confident that Jackie had administered mixtures of Tylenol and multiple vitamins – and at least on one occasion he had seen her offer Reso part of an orange. In any event, he protested, feeding their victim was a woman's work.

The two kidnappers did not agree as to how their victim had died. According to Jackie, Reso had expired overnight in the wooden box; when they visited the storage locker on Sunday morning, 3 May, and opened the box, Reso was already grey and motionless. Arthur Seale, on the other hand, said that when they arrived on that Sunday morning, Reso was still alive: they could hear him 'speaking' through the box, despite the duct-tape that bound his lips. Seale had opened the box and noticed that their prisoner seemed paler and weaker than on the day before. He had sat Reso up on the edge of the box, holding him from behind, and attempted external heart-massage. Reso had shuddered, the sound of liquid could be heard in his mouth, and he had died in his kidnapper's arms.

It was with an odd persistence that Seale defended his version of Reso's last moments, as if he believed that his timely embrace of his dying victim entitled him to mercy, if not at the hands of his judges, at least in the minds of the viewing public. If that was the prisoner's calculation, he was wrong, for nobody who watched the television interview would have ranked Arthur Seale with Florence Nightingale.

The Ice-Cream Gang Cometh

RICHARD WHITTINGTON-EGAN

A BALMY WEST COAST June day in 1992. After a 54-day trial – Scotland's longest in a criminal cause – on charges involving drug-dealing and its orbital satellites, murder, attempted murder and kneecapping, the twenty-eight-year-old Glasgow hard man stands, surrounded by an immobilized phalanx of certainly not laughing 'polis' men, on the Justiciary Court House steps. Arms outstretched like a missionary about to emit a benediction, his shrewd eyes survey the scene of his freshly-laundered triumph. Look, he has come through the judicial cleansing machine; emerged clean as a whistle, Sanforised by fifteen men good and true. The cameras click like rapid-fire false teeth in a film-star burst of flashes. Vindicated, jury-certificated upright citizen, Paul Ferris 'smiled twice', as they have it in Glaswegian parlance – once like everyone else, then an involuntary encore presented by the 'chib' memorial scar, snaking from the right side of an ungenerously lipped mouth to the shadow below a firm-set jaw-line. A final significant gesture . . . Then it was off to a champagne-supper celebration.

No corks popping, though, for the almost biblically nicknamed Blind Jonah, only thirty-six, his face described variously as 'a hot cross-bun of knife-work,' and 'a sort of flesh map of the gang battles of Glasgow.' Mr Jonah McKenzie is a walking object-lesson in survival. Not that he walks too well after the knife attack that severed the leg muscles. Reputedly one of Young Arthur's Team, aka the Thompson Gang, the opposition to Mr Ferris's Barlanark Team, he is said, by Mr Ferris, to have brought a great many of his troubles on himself, by lending a hand in the murder of Arthur Thompson, Junior, and by kneecapping William Gillen, a Barlanark aide. Blind Jonah has been made the (head) butt of unfeeling hard-man humour:

> Question: What kind of weapon does Blind Jonah use?
> Answer: A Braille gun.

No fizzy either at Mr Ferris's festal free-for-all for Limpy Willie Gillen aforesaid, a turncoat Barlanarkian barnacle who had the rash temerity to nominate his whilom boss as his kneecapper. Not so, said Mr Ferris's jury.

And there was no celebrating at locally dubbed 'South-fork', two stone-cladded-into-one council houses, garnished with Spanish patio, satellite dish and refined ornatures of that ilk: the Provanmill Road home of the man they call the Godfather of Glasgow, Arthur Thompson, Senior, whose thirty-one-year-old son, 'Young Arthur,' aka 'Fat Boy', was into wholesale heroin as a dealer before being dealt out by a blowaway job – fatally shot while enjoying an innocuous weekend furlough from an eleven stretch in jail. The jury had likewise pronounced seven-times-libelled Mr Ferris unconnected with this sad event.

Who wiped out the Fat Boy? Melted him down? Echo answers who. But, deservedly or undeservedly, two hard men of Mr Ferris's Barlanark Team, Joe 'Bananas' Hanlon and Bobby Glover, were scythed down by the grim reaper on the very morning of Young Arthur's funeral. Bananas and Bobby stood not upon the order of their going. In point of fact, they lay, cherubic, side by side, death did not divide them, in their car, parked outside the earthly valhalla of a favourite pub, twin bullet holes in the napes of their necks and, for good measure and as a reminder (to others) of the importance of rectitude, even in a life

21

of crime, a carefully aimed bullet apiece up the rectum.

Both the Thompsons and the Ferrises hail from Blackhill, an abysmally drear scheme (*écossais* for Council Estate) to the north-east of the city centre. Thompson, Senior, is a man with a chequered past – convictions for assault, housebreaking, robbery, safe-blowing and extortion – which he does not deny. But, for nearly a quarter of a century now, Mr Thompson has steered well clear of little malfeasances of the sort in which he had permitted himself to indulge in the 1960s. Standing, in recent times, below the security camera limpeted upon the stucco of his fortress home, he pooh-poohed the notion of his being the Glasgow Godfather. 'I would have to start talking like Don Corleone,' he chaffed merrily, adding, with less twinkle, 'It's pure nonsense.'

As the 1980s mounted, so did the spiral of violence. The temperatures of the participating factions climbed way out of control. It was in 1985 that Young Arthur had been sentenced to eleven years for trafficking in heroin. While he was inside, battle had to be joined for the preservation of his outside trading territory. A first major indication of the flaring of the drug war came when, in 1986, Old Arthur was wounded in the groin while innocently tinkering with his motor. For the record: in 1989 Young Arthur's sister, Margaret, died with a heroin needle in her arm – a cruel irony which brings no moralizing gratification in its wake.

Drug rivalries came bursting, literally, into the open in 1990, when a hand grenade was rolled into the pub where Ferris's Barlanarks did their drinking. Hard on the heels of that, Arthur Thompson, Senior, was put into hospital after being the victim of a most determined hit-and-run car accident.

Repercussively, Paul Ferris's father, Willie, a cripple already, who walked with two sticks, came in for some pretty rough handling with hammer, baseball bat and razor. Following one such attack he had more than a

22

hundred stitches. His tyres were slashed and his car with its 'disabled' label subsequently torched.

Torched, too, was Joe 'Bananas' Hanlon's ice-cream van, salespoint also for heroin. And later his XR2 was blown up and he was shot in the penis.

Then, in August 1990, came the rubbing out of Young Arthur and the consequent erasure – or execution – of Joe and Bobby.

Hard-line humour:

> Question: What is the favourite song on Glasgow's karaoke machines?
> Answer: Yes, we have Joe Bananas.

It took three bullets to fell Arthur Thomson, Junior. Number one nicked his cheek. Number two chipped his ribs. Number three hit bang smack home in his heart. Famous last words, to his sister: 'I've been shot, hen. I'm going to collapse.'

The whisper is that a £30,000 contract is out on Ferris.

Hard-folk joke:

> Question: What's the difference between Paul Ferris and Elvis Presley?
> Answer: Paul Ferris is definitely dead.

Mr Ferris himself treats this maleficent ribaldry with all the contempt an innocent man naturally feels for such manipulative fat-chewing.

And yet . . . Glasgow is no kingdom of empty threats. Dark promises are kept, bloody vendettas kept up. The plain truth is that this roaring nineties Runyonland north of the Border preserves the ancient order – or, rather, *dis*order – hymned by that thirties prose bard of the Gorbals, A. McArthur, and his *No Mean City* accomplice, H. Kingsley Long.

Who today knows anything of McArthur, the little Gorbals grocer who set himself the task of immortalizing the blood-frothed spilth and sport of the razor gangs of his local streets, and succeeded in it so magnificently?

23

Not great literature, but he produced a wondrously powerful manuscript – no mean feat considering his tenuous literacy – which, after being shorn of sundry stylistic quiddities and licked into grammatical shape by the co-author, very likely a relative of his London publisher, John Long, *No Mean City*, published in 1936, became a bestseller. It has to date sold upwards of 17 million copies. McArthur set to – with a co-author again – hoping to repeat his success with a sequel, *No Bad Money*. Sadly, there was to be no second small miracle. What modest confidence McArthur had built up in his writing ability pitifully swiftly drained away. Depressed, he pitifully swiftly drained away the contents of far too many bottles. They found him dead on the banks of the Clyde, full of methylated spirits.

But the gangs of Glasgow had come into being a good half-century before McArthur began his basically accurate but, even so, highly-coloured, chroniclings. The first named collection of organized Glaswegian hooligans to take shape out of the fogs and rain-mists of the remoter reaches of the past was the Penny Mob, who were brawling around the Townhead district in the 1880s. This earliest, recorded as such, gang, numbered about three hundred, and took its name from the fact that every member had to chip in a penny a week to a kitty which provided money for the payment of fines imposed on members of the mob by the courts. The leaders of the Penny Mob packs were known, rather oddly, as 'Chairmen' – the title bestowed upon them actually in court reports of the time. The Penny Mobsmen would be encountered lolling on street corners, prowling among the sprawling East End tenements looking for mischief, and making nuisances of themselves in and around city pubs. Quite a sizeable proportion of Penny Mob violence was, it seems, the Dead Sea fruit of religious intolerance.

The next collection of unworthies to figure with any prominence on the Glasgow roll of dishonour were those young turn-of-the-century tearaways, aged mainly between sixteen and twenty, who banded themselves together in gangs of a hundred or more under such bizarre banners as the Hi Hi, operating in the Northern Police Division area; the Ping Pong, in the Eastern Division; and the San Toy, the Tim Malloy, the South Side Stickers, and the Village Boys in the Southern District. These gangs attached great importance to territoriality, identifying themselves with specific tracts and sections of the city which they regarded as their exclusive preserves. The San Toy Boys, particular rivals of the Penny Mob, came from Calton, rather nearer to the city centre. Extremely belligerent, their war-cry as they charged into street battle was: 'We are the young Santoys and we can fight the Tim Malloys.'

None of the early twentieth-century gang members carried razors, knives or bicycle chains. They were weaponed up with knuckle-dusters, heavy, old-fashioned bolts shaped like small, lethal dumb-bells, a brass rod with a hefty doorknob at the end, and, a great favourite this, a small poker carried hidden up the sleeve.

The young gangsters would waylay folk coming out of places of entertainment and demand money with menaces, go into shops for cigarettes and public-houses for drinks, all to be handed over, of course, without payment.

Whatever, with ego-boosting grandiloquence, they called themselves, the hooligans were originally known to everyone else in Glasgow as 'Keelies' – a Keelie is defined in the Scots dictionary as 'a street-arab; a pickpocket' – but for many years now the name has been changed to 'neds'. No one seems to remember how or when the term originated. The dictionary definition is: 'a donkey, a simpleton.'

In the years leading up to the Great War, the Glasgow gangs proliferated. The Redskins was one exceptionally vicious gang, numbering among its members several young girls, one of whom was the legendary and truly formidable Aggie Reid, who lived in a women's hostel in Trongate. Her record of arrests for assault was both long and alarming. It took at least four policemen to get her into a van. Boasting an organized membership of a thousand, the Redskins took over the East End, vanquishing the Hi Hi and the Calton Black Hand, and seeing off also the Hazel Bells from Mile End and Bridgeton, the Baltic Fleet from Baltic Street, and the Kelly Boys from Govan.

Fisticuff fighting was despised. Battle was waged preferably with meat-cleavers. Failing that, with hammers. Protection money was extracted from shopkeepers and other tradesmen, and the gangs did not think twice about openly attacking and robbing people in the street in broad daylight. Leaders were no longer 'Chairmen' but 'Kings', and there were also 'Queens', invariably the prettiest, and not uncommonly the wildest, under-twenty-ones. If any Redskin found him or herself in trouble, a special loud, quick, tuneless whistle would bring rapid relief reinforcements.

Throughout the Great War (1914–18), gangland activity subsided. There was fighting of a different kind to be done; a new arena for the channelling of brute energies. Meanwhile, for those keeping the home fires burning, peak production demands at the shipyards and in the munition factories reduced that unemployment out of which street violence and idle-hands villainy had arisen and been recruited.

With the war's end, however, all the old spectres – unrequited slumland hunger and thirst, dizzy new heights of unemployment – stalked the streets where the surviving heroes who had fought to make Scotland a land fit for heroes to live in, sold matches and boot-laces. So, ill-shod feet came marching back to the sounding of drumbeats calling up the old troops of Redskins and Calton Black Handers, and conscripting willing new 'soldiers' to new gangs which would replace those which, through loss of leadership, attrition due to the passage of time and war, had simply dwindled away. And gradually the hoodlum body was revitalized. In his memoirs, *Life Begins at Midnight*, the late Detective

Chief Superintendent Robert Colquhoun remembered 1923 as a vintage year for Glasgow's gangs. The Cheeky Forty and the Black Diamonds were his very particular *bêtes noires* in his bailiwick, St Rollox. Elsewhere in the town, he says, the Redskins, the Norman Conks and the Billy Boys were entrenched, and a new outfit, the Beehives, was just beginning to buzz.

Three more names to conjure with.

The hostility between the Norman Conks (unexpectedly erudite corruption of William the Norman Conqueror in conjunction with the fact that the gang's headquarters was in Norman Street explains the nomenclature) and the Billy Boys, more prosaically doffing their nominal caps to that other King William, of Orange, aka King Billy, both stomping the East End, was a matter more than territorial. Glasgow, it must be understood, and many things Glaswegian, are shot through with the steel thread of religion. It goes back to the impact upon the native Protestant Scots of Irish Catholic immigrant workers, brought over at the time of the Industrial Revolution. The old rivalry survives, even though the initial cause of that rivalry has diminished as religion withers nationally. It was former Chief Constable of Glasgow, Sir David McNee, who said that one of his senior officers described the football matches between green-shirted, Catholic Celtic, from the East End, and blue-shirted, Protestant Rangers, from the South, as 'the biggest outdoor religious festival held anywhere in the world.'

The Norman Conks were led by a ferocious character named 'Bull' Bowman, under whose sanguineous command they ported their favourite arms, 42-inch-long pick-shafts, weighing close on three pounds, backed up by a variegated weaponry of swords, hatchets, and lovingly sharpened bicycle chains, worn like a rosary round the necks of their Queens, because they knew the police hesitated to search girls for fear of accusations of improper assault. For hand-to-hand infighting, beer bottles were the first choice. Favourite target of these favourite weapons were, of course, the Billy Boys.

The Billy Boys' boss was William (Billy) Fullerton, who used to work in Gilmour's Club in Olympia Street, Bridgeton. The gang, eight hundred strong, had kept up the Penny Mob tradition of exacting a weekly payment and, allowing no doubt for inflation, a tuppence per week contribution was marked up on all membership cards. The resultant nest-egg, tucked safely away in the local bank, provided funds for fines and also for the bringing of small comforts to wives whose men were, for reasons not unconnected with the courts, temporarily out of circulation. At one stage the nest-egg, to which, incidentally, local shopkeepers were also 'invited' to donate, topped well in excess of £1,200, and Fullerton lifted about half of this sum to kit out a flute-and-drum band. Rabid Orangemen, the Billy Boys were henceforth able to taunt the Catholic arch-enemy by marching down Norman Street on Saints' and Holy Days, fluting and drumming lusty Orange airs. The Conks' religious response was a hail of pick-shafts, bricks, bottles and bucketfuls of ordure. The tale is still told of how on one such occasion, when things had really got out of hand and attracted a full-scale charge of mounted police, a quick-thinking Billy Boy, Elijah Cooper, took a smart header into the big drum he had been beating and rolled off hidden therein to avoid the drumming hooves of the police steeds.

The Beehive Corner Boys – so christened after their meeting-place, subsequently abbreviated to the Bee-hive Gang – developed along different lines from most of the other gangs, whose main objects were to display ego-building machismo to their Queens, maintain a firm hold on their territory, and bash, slash and generally mutilate a respectable quota of the enemy. To them, heavy crime was incidental, happenstance, peripheral. To the misbehaving Beehives, however, serious crime was very much an integral part of their agenda. Thieving, housebreaking, shopbreaking, safe-blowing, hold-up jobs and intimidation were all on the menu;

28

which meant that the Beehive was thus posing a greater threat to the respectable citizenry.

Beehive organization was, moreover, formidable – almost army fashion – with young recruits enlisting in the cadet branch, earning promotion to auxiliary membership and final enrolment to the hard, inner core attained only after success in various tests and trials.

Weaponry: razors, hatchets, chains and bottles.
Footwear: fighting boots with carpenter's nails projecting wickedly from the toe-caps.
Headgear: cap with razor-blade stitched in the peak.

Their King was Peter Williamson, powerfully built, in his early twenties, a legend in his own lifetime, as the cliché has it, for his prowess with his fists. Second in command was his friend, Harry McMenemy. The real mastermind was said to be a character named Howie.

The Beehive did not survive the Second World War. Peter Williamson did. He went into the army and was soon made up to sergeant. Demobbed, he returned to Glasgow . . . and safe-blowing . . . and Peterhead Prison.

The Beehive territory was especially the Cumberland Street area of the Gorbals, and by 1931, when, following his gang-busting success in Sheffield, my good friend Sir Percy Sillitoe was appointed Chief Constable of Glasgow, the Beehives were the undoubted rulers of their chosen domain.

Over the preceding decade, the gangland scene had undergone inevitable changes. The Billy Boys were still in there, battling away against the Norman Conks. Also in the East End were the Romeo Boys, the San Toy and its Gallowgate subsidiary the Bridgegate Boys, the Stickit Boys and the Derry Boys from Bridgeton and the Antique Mob from Shettleston. The legions from the South Side numbered among them the Black Diamond Boys, the Hammer Boys and the Dirty Dozen. Govan contributed the Kelly-bow. A state of open warfare was disastrously ongoing between the South Side Stickers and the San Toy Boys.

The Parlour Boys – so called because their head-quarters was the Bedford Parlour Dance Hall in Celtic Street – was another of the smaller, but perilous to ignore, gangs. Their leader, twenty-six-year-old James 'Razzle-Dazzle' Dalziel, was so self-consciously macho that he sneered at dancing with girls as effeminate, and would only take the floor with another burly male member of the gang.

In the Glasgow of the 1930s, it was a case of one thing laughing at another, for while, civic pride in full swell, 'Glesca toon' was boasting, and boosting, itself as the Second City of the British Empire, life for the painful majority was no picnic in the grim valley of the Clyde. One man in three was out of work. Times were rough and things got rougher.

It was the Gorbals that in these years introduced a new weapon to the skirmish scene – the open razor. The phrase 'razor-slashing' started to appear in the public prints. The regular pitched-battles for transient supremacy raged. Pathetic, cloth-capped young men, the losers, were carted off, bloodstained bundles, to lock-up or casualty. Older, more cunning men, veteran survivors of the war to end wars, began, first to infiltrate, and then to take command of the war to end want – their personal want – on the crustless streets. The gang battles, the internecine warrings, escalated to pretty terrifying proportions. Gurkha knives and bayonets were added to the armoury; souvenirs, no doubt, in some cases, of previous combative engagements overseas.

Sillitoe countered with an even rougher offensive. Using without compunction the toughest men in his force, on the poacher-turned-gamekeeper principle, he had them conveyed under cover, in furniture vans and suchlike inconspicuous transports, to the site of the hasslings and there unleashed them with wink-as-good-as-a-nod permission to bring to play whatever exercise of strength they liked to sanitize the streets. And Sillitoe

30

was winning when, in 1939, the Second World War interrupted his street-gang sweeping campaign. He relinquished his Chief Constableship in 1943.

The 1939–45 war that coffined and buried so many of the old ways, good and bad, brought in its wake changes of catastrophic dimension. Socialist City Fathers occupying the chambers of civic power decreed a New Order for auld Glasgie. The noisome, festering, massively overcrowded old sandstone tenement slums – the Glasgow ghettos, McArthur's Land – were to be razed. Bulldozers should do what the blitz did not. New schemes 'amid the green hills far away' on the virgin fringes of the city. Bright new dormitories for the deserving. But the idealists should have listened and been warned. Did not their own national poet caution, 'The best laid schemes . . . Gang aft a-gley'? And these, it has with hindsight to be admitted, were not the best. Oh, the houses, acres and acres of look-alike, balconied grey battleships breasting the green wave-crests of the circumjacent hills, were fine. Nothing a-gley there; the baths and indoor toilets were all present and correct, the paint was bright, the wallpaper cheery, roofs watertight. But, and it was a very big but, the enthusiastic, well-intentioned planners forgot to graft a heart into the place. Essentials, basic and more, had been remembered and supplied, but amenities had been forgotten. No places of sport or entertainment had been laid on. There was even a dearth of shops. Bus services to the city centre were poor. Boredom and depression became the next-door neighbours of the inhabitants of the new, cut off, Robinson Crusoe townships. Easterhouse, Drumchapel, Castlemilk and Pollok . . . the names droop off the tongue like a litany of despair. Here, in this concrete and chrome heaven turned to hell, was a splendid new breeding ground for the fresh gangs. Meanwhile, those left behind – those not yet included in, and encompassed by, the rural–urban drift – found idle hands' solution to relieve the novel boredom and frustration. The inner city infra-structure might be crumbling but, despite decimated territories and depopulated streets, it was still tough enough to support a thinning scatter of gangs, whose members, in their bewilderment at the disintegration of the environment and cognate eco-system, sought security of identification in the redoubling of self-expressive violence.

So it was that, in the late 1950s, the old, if not venerable, Glasgow tradition of street gangs and territorial violence came back with a terrible new vivacity. Even more disturbing was the speedy revelation that the use of the considerably more lethal knife had replaced the horribly mutilating but far less life-threatening razor as the weapon wielded with a new ruthless disregard for fatal consequence.

The gang names, new names, started to appear. Alongside the Tongs from Townhead, the Cumbie from the Gorbals, the Fleet from Maryhill, the Govan Team, there came the Buck and the Drummie from Drumchapel, the Toi and the Young Team from Castlemilk, the Bal Toi, the Torran Toi and the Bar L (named after Barlinnie Prison) from Easterhouse, and the Shamrock from Blackhill – that same Blackhill which spawned the Thompsons and the Ferrises.

The wings of the new breed of hoodlums were well clipped by Lord Cameron and his fellow-judges at the High Court, who handed out hefty exemplary sentences. But the containment of the mayhem and the ferocity was destined to be utterly shattered by the emergence in the early sixties of the drug problem. This was to become so grievous and far-reaching in its consequences, especially among the young, that the increase of other crimes – such as the opening up of local shebeens, illegal money-lending at extortionate interest rates, as well as the traditional bread-and-butter villainies of theft and protection racketeering – paled.

The 1970s and 1980s have witnessed a dramatic upsurge in the statistics of murder and serious assaults committed by gang members, although, oddly, the number of weapon-bearing gangs actually out on the streets has decreased.

The first half of the 1980s will always be remembered for the ferocious Glasgow Ice-Cream Wars, and their terrible culmination in what has been frequently described as Scotland's most horrific mass murder. Despite the long and strongly whispered rumour that drugs were at the back of it all, the best authority – and I am including in this the statement of the campaigning journalists Douglas Skelton and Lisa Brownlie, the authors of *Frightener* (1992), a close-focus study of the ice-cream scene – denies this. At the root of the trouble was the good, old-fashioned, Thatcherite profit motive gone obscenely wrong.

In order to understand, which is not to say to sympathize with, the market pressures leading to inevitable commercial battlings, all one needs to appreciate is that the struggle was for control of the 'runs' or sales pitches of the numerous ice-cream vans operating on the various council estates. These sales of ice-cream, sweeties, soft drinks, crisps and cigarettes were not peanuts. Without over-exerting yourself, you could rake in profits ranging between £200 and £800 a week, the higher figure if you were prepared to reset (receive) stolen wares.

Theoretically, anybody could enter into this free enterprise. There were two routes: you could buy your own van and pay to garage it at the premises of such cash-and-carry firms as Fifti Ices, who would also sell you stock, or you could lease a van by the week. If you chose the latter course, you had a choice of three hire firms – the Marchetti Brothers, Capaldi & Sons, and the Viking Ice-Cream Company. You would pay £50 to £60 a week for the vehicle, the hire company being responsible for all the costs, other than petrol, of keeping the van on the road; that is to say, maintenance, insurance, tax and so on.

As realization of the rich pickings to be had from this nice little earner dawned, insalubrious interests were raised, insalubrious characters muscled in, and feuding over the best runs broke out. Each side was, according to the police, backed by well-known criminals. Out came the balaclava-ed strong-arm men, wielding baseball bats and shotguns, and fifty-seven varieties of scare tactics were put into force, including discretionary torchings.

The ultimate torching was the setting on fire, in the small hours of Monday, 16 April 1984, of the top-floor flat of No 29 Bankend Street, in the district of Ruchazie, where Andrew Doyle, eighteen-year-old driver of an ice-cream van put on to the disputed Garthamlock run by Marchetti, lived. Six people perished, including Andrew and an eighteen-month-old baby.

The gangland boss identified as responsible by the police was thirty-one-year-old Thomas Campbell, a hard man's hard man known shuddersomely throughout the underworld as 'T. C'. His lieutenant in the matter was said to be Joseph Steele, hitherto qualifying as nothing more nefarious than a petty thief. Tried in September 1984, these two received life sentences. But there are those, the authors of *Frightener* among them, who believe that Campbell and Steele are the victims of a miscarriage of justice. This does not *necessarily* imply innocence – indeed, the word on the street at the time was that they were guilty – but what it does suggest is that, innocent or guilty of the act libelled, the position is unacceptable if false evidence was used to secure the convictions. A key prosecution witness, William Love, has sworn an affidavit that he lied at the Glasgow High Court trial. An independent public inquiry into the way the police investigated the Doyle murders is currently being sought.

What, one may ask, is the outlook for Glasgow, erstwhile City of European Culture, city with a drink problem three times as high as anywhere else in Britain and generally acknowledged to be the alcoholic capital of Western Europe –

Hard-folk joke:

Question: What is Glasgow's favourite drink?
Answer: Kneecappuccino.

– home to 900,000, of whom 12,500 are main-lining H (for Heroin, not Hard) men and women, and addicts of a hotchpotch of other junk for junkies? More than somewhat unhealthy.

There's only one way out: gang up on the drug gangs.

Two Sides to a Question

SOMETIMES THERE IS MORE – or less – to a story than meets certain press reporters' eyes; and, of course, some reporters – and some newspapers, not exclusively of the tabloid kind – are loathe to let facts get in the way of a good story. The saying, 'Never mind the quality, feel the width,' has always applied to the editing of radio and television news programmes, for the editors of such programmes are more concerned with piecing together a menu of items that fills a seconds-exact time-slot than with checking that each of the items contains about the right amounts of the right ingredients. Also, in recent years the moguls of news broadcasting have blurred the distinction between The Reporter and The Commentator, to the extent that it is now common to hear a reporter, just arrived in some foreign place where he has never been before, airing his opinions on, and even prophesying outcomes of, whatever happenings have made his journey seem necessary.

In October 1992, there was a flurry of shock-horror reports in the British news media concerning a long-running, still-running murder case in Hawaii, the string of islands that makes up a State of the American Union, which is rarely mentioned in British papers other than on pages devoted to holiday travel. I have taken the liberty of combining the published reports I have seen, leaving out repetition and padding:

'British consular officials are investigating the case of Malcolm Greyson, a Briton held for nine years in a Hawaiian jail and now awaiting his fifth trial on the same murder charge. Merrick Baker-Bates, the British

Consul-General in Los Angeles, has protested to the Honolulu chief prosecutor, Keith Kaneshiro, and asked for an explanation.

'Greyson, born in Margate, Kent, left Britain with his parents in 1956, when he was five. He later travelled in South America and then, from 1975, spent eight years surfing in Hawaii. His wife left him after his arrest and returned to her native Bolivia. His parents live in California.

'He was arrested in 1983 and charged with murdering his seven-month-old son Eric. Prosecutors say he hit the child, causing an abdominal injury from which he died. But Greyson says he stepped on the boy accidentally and immediately took him to hospital, where he died because of inexcusable delays and medical errors.

'Each of his four previous court appearances in Honolulu have ended in mistrials. At his first trial, in 1984, he was convicted by a judge sitting without a jury and was sentenced to fifteen years' imprisonment. The conviction was overturned by the Hawaii Supreme Court. His second trial, in 1986, resulted in a hung jury. A year later, a jury convicted him, but the verdict was again overturned by the Supreme Court because of "prosecutorial misconduct". His fourth trial, in August 1992, was another mistrial, as the jury could not decide on the degree of the hospital's responsibility for the boy's death. His situation has since been further complicated because he has been accused of masterminding a conspiracy to smuggle in cocaine in hollowed-out electric guitars to raise bail money. He says these charges are ludicrous.

'Myles Breiner, Greyson's court-appointed lawyer, says: "He is the only person in US history to be tried five times on the same charge. The trials have already cost the taxpayers a million dollars. He is a thorn in the side of the Hawaiian prosecutors, and they seem determined to get a conviction, no matter how many trials it takes. They keep re-trying him with the same witnesses and the same evidence. They could go on for the rest of his life. The ironic thing is that if his original fifteen-year sentence had not been overturned, he'd be out by now."

'The murder case has become a talking point on the island of Oahu [on which Honolulu is situated]. A local television station ran a poll of viewers which was overwhelmingly against another trial.

'Greyson, interviewed in jail, says: "I am an intelligent human being whose life is wasting away in prison just because the Hawaiian prosecutors don't want to lose face. I'm being persecuted."

'Douglas Woo, the chief prosecutor's special assistant, says: "If Mr Greyson is not convicted at the next trial, we will evaluate the situation and, if necessary, try him again."'

Wondering if the reports were accurate, I sent copies of them to Kevin K. Takata, the deputy prosecuting attorney for the City and County of Honolulu who handled the fourth trial, and he replied as follows:

'Malcolm Greyson was twice convicted of murder, once by a judge and once by a jury, and at the other two trials the jury was unable to act unanimously, being split 11–1 and 10–2 for murder.

'The murder occurred in February 1983, and Greyson was extradited back to Honolulu in February 1984 because he ran away to California. Since 1988, Greyson has asked for and been granted numerous continuances to prepare for trial, while the State has always been ready and not sought any continuances.

'The excuses offered by Greyson for his infant son's death began with a story that the child ate "bad carrots," progressed to a fall from a two-feet-high bed on to a small toy, developed to Greyson leaping off the bed to answer the phone and stepping on his son, and culminated in a claim that the treating doctors killed the child. This last claim was made despite the fact that the fatal injury, which Greyson admits inflicting, was so severe that it severed the infant's intestines against his spine, and Greyson then waited over three hours before seeking medical attention.

'Upon arriving at the hospital, the child was blue, unresponsive, and barely breathing. The emergency-room doctor acted immediately to resuscitate him, then transported him to a nearby hospital that specializes in the care of infants. Surgery was performed to repair the severed intestines and torn spleen. The child's condition was so bad that no anaesthesia was used because it might have caused cardiac arrest. The following day, the infant died from his injuries.

'Greyson claims he loved his son. However, during surgery a doctor explained to him how badly injured his son was and Greyson's response was: "That's OK, we can have another one."

'To support his medical malpractice claim, Greyson hired a doctor whose medical licence was suspended after he was convicted for distributing cocaine and whose licence was revoked after a patient died following a minor, routine procedure; this same doctor was asked to leave several hospitals.

'The articles you sent contain numerous false statements that I would like to set straight. First, Mr Merrick Baker-Bates did not protest to Keith Kaneshiro, the chief prosecutor. I was present during the meeting, and Mr Baker-Bates made it perfectly clear that his purpose was not to advocate for Greyson but rather to gather information on the background and status of the case.

'Second, there have been two mistrials, not four. When a jury is unable to act unanimously, the judge declares a mistrial. The fourth trial ended in a mistrial not because the jury could not decide on the hospital's responsibility for the infant's death, but because two jurors disagreed with the definition of murder, so they refused to convict Greyson of murder!

'Third, no poll was conducted by anyone to determine how people felt about another trial.

'Myles Breiner, attorney for Greyson, claims that Greyson is the only person in the United States to be tried five times, and claims that the trials have cost one million dollars. I don't know where Breiner gets his information from, but it is obvious he has trouble with numbers. For he states that Greyson got a fifteen-year prison-term following the first trial and that if that judgment had not been overturned, Greyson would be a free man now. Even if Greyson had been incarcerated in 1983, which he was not because he ran away and was not picked up until the following year, a fifteen-year prison-term would carry him to the year 1998.

'Murder is a heinous enough crime as it is, but it is even more so when the victim is an infant. Greyson claims his life is wasting away in prison, but what of his infant son who never got to enjoy boyhood and grow into a man?'

Greyson's fifth trial for the murder of his son, scheduled for May 1993, was postponed because he again appealed the case. The appeal having been denied by the Hawaii Supreme Court, the case was sent back to the trial court – but at the time of going to press (October 1993), no trial date has been set, the reason for the further delay being that Greyson has filed motions that must be resolved beforehand. Meanwhile, however, Greyson has been convicted in the federal court of conspiring to import cocaine; he awaits sentencing for that crime, which may add fifteen years to his imprisonment. It appears that, whatever the result of his fifth trial for murder, he is destined to remain in Hawaii, probably shuttling between a prison and one appeal court or another, for a considerable time to come.

An Appointment with Death

LYNNE ROGERS WAS SEVENTEEN when she died, which was in the early part of September 1991, on or soon after the fourth day of that month. The exact date of her death is not known, and probably never will be.

Of slight build, proud of her curly auburn hair, which she had let grow long, well past shoulder-length, she was known as a 'get-up-and-go sort of girl' to her many friends in Catford, the part of south-east London where she lived with her parents and her older sister Suzanne. Even before she left school, she had expressed determinations about what she was going to do with her life, and in the few months since, while working at a local office, she had used much of her spare time towards realizing the first of her objectives – to get a job as a courier, or something of that sort, with an overseas-travel firm. By the end of August, she had written about a hundred letters, either in answer to sits-vac advertisements or on the offchance; few of the firms had bothered to reply, and none of those had even offered an interview.

But then a man phoned the house, asking to talk to her. Suzanne, who took the call, said that Lynne was out, and offered to take a message. She gathered from voices in the background – men speaking briefly and precisely, and as if into microphones, of things like compass-bearings, flight paths and runway numbers – that the caller was in an air-traffic-control office. He said that he was in the travel business, that he was looking for someone like Lynne to accompany businessmen to places in Europe. He declined to leave a message, but having asked when

Lynne would be at home, said that he would ring again.

He did. Afterwards, Lynne was excited – and confident that the job was hers. She told her family, her boyfriend too, that she had to meet the man, of course, but simply to arrange when she was to start – at a salary of £14,500, three times what she was presently earning! She had offered to meet 'her new boss' wherever and whenever was convenient to him, and he, having looked at his diary, had said that he was going to be in London, at Charing Cross Station, on the morning of Wednesday the fourth. Before he could have second thoughts, she had said that she would be at a particular place on the station at a particular time.

It couldn't have been more convenient for her, because trains from Catford Bridge Station go direct to Charing Cross. She arrived early. She was wearing her best clothes. She went into a toilet to check that they hadn't got creased, that there were no smudges to her make-up (yes, exactly the right small amount, Suzanne had assured and reassured her), that her freshly-washed hair was tidy. Still with time to spare, she made her way to the area beneath the clock. At least one person noticed her. Shortly afterwards, outside the station, others noticed her getting into a blue car with a man in a black suit. It appears that, apart from the man who would kill her, those bystanders were the last people to see her alive.

Four days later, dreadful days for her family and friends, her corpse was found in brambles beside a lane near the village of Rotherfield, in East Sussex. She had been strangled. A bite-mark on her chin suggested a sexual motive for the crime, but there was no evidence of rape. As it had not rained for some time, the ground near the brambles was hard, showing no footprints. Scientific examination of the girl's clothes (in the pockets of which were, among other things, her return train ticket and her purse, which contained cash) revealed extraneous fibres, but none that was out of the ordinary.

During the previous couple of days, following press

42

reports of her disappearance, people who recalled seeing her either at or near Charing Cross Station had come forward, and so the police already had two leads, very slender ones: a blue car, a black-suited driver. Now a Rotherfield farmer said that he had recently seen a blue car parked half a mile from where the body was found. He hadn't the faintest idea of the make – but he had glanced at the registration plate, and (this must have astonished the policemen he spoke to) still remembered most of its letters and digits. The investigators enlisted the help of the vehicle licensing authority in Scrabble-like efforts to identify the car.

Those efforts were soon focused upon cars owned by men living in Crawley, the first major town to the west of Rotherfield, and about thirty miles south of London. The reason for the focusing was that the Crawley police had received information from a local woman: she said that, while shopping on a day just prior to Lynne Rogers's disappearance, she, waiting to use a public phone, had eavesdropped on the man who was using it – had heard him offering a job with an air-travel company that he claimed to own. She had taken no notice of him – or rather, of his back, all she saw of him – and had only remembered the incident because of her irritation at the misuse of a scarce public phone for office business.

A list of local men who had cars fitting within the description was narrowed down to those, only a few, with criminal records. All but one of the men on the short list had a secure alibi for Wednesday, 4 September. The odd man out was known by two names. The name on his birth certificate, which also showed that his father was German, his mother English, was André Paul Reich, but within the past few months, since reaching the age of thirty-five, he had officially become Wayne Scott Paul Singleton – Scott Singleton for short.

He was of medium build, pasty-faced, sleepy-eyed; he had dark, lacklustre hair, untidy around a bald pate, and wore a moustache, sometimes a beard as well; most of

43

his clothes were of the casual sort, but he had a black suit for special occasions.

Though a trained car-mechanic, he had often been unemployed, and was now. Earlier in the summer, he had given up trying to make a success of a one-man motor-repair shop at a commercial complex in Greenwich, south-east London. His longest period of continuous employment seems to have been three years at the end of the 1980s, when he was a carpenter at Gatwick Airport, close to Crawley. Having left that job, perhaps not voluntarily, he obtained money from a news-paper by telling shock-horror stories about lax security at the airport; he said that, though he had committed crimes, including grievous bodily harm, 'within twenty minutes of arriving to start work, I was issued with a pass which gave me unlimited access. I have turned my back on crime now, but . . . I could have been tempted for cash to carry a bomb on to a plane.'

It is unlikely that he would have remained working at the airport for a comparatively long time had he not been fascinated, some would say obsessed, with aviation. When he was twenty-one, he had started to learn to fly, but had hardly got off the ground before being expelled from the school for non-payment of fees. Lately, he had joined an Essex flying club, where he was already known as that boring fellow who always insisted upon doing an impersonation, admittedly very good, of a flight controller coping with a Mayday call. While he was still running the motor-repair business at Greenwich, he had exchanged an American sports-car that worked for a microlight aircraft that didn't. The disjointed parts of the small machine additionally littered his unkempt home, a council house in a part of Crawley called Wilkinson Court.

He had lived alone in the house since 1986, when his wife had left him, taking with her the two children born early on in the eleven-year marriage. Though he had had a daughter by a girlfriend in 1989, his wife had never divorced him, and he visited her quite often. In recent months, however, he had seen far less of her than of a woman named Kim Arnold, who lived with her three children in Catford, close to the house belonging to the Rogers family.

A geographical coincidence, perhaps.

The police had, of course, interviewed members of the Rogers family, Suzanne in particular, soon after Lynne's father, Derek, had reported her disappearance. Following the discovery of her body, other detectives, members of the East Sussex force, went to the house in the hope of jogging Suzanne's memory of the phone call, of any peculiarity in the way the caller spoke – and also (unhopefully, just as a matter of routine) to look through Lynne's 'JOB HUNT' folder.

There were all sorts of papers in the folder: clippings of travel firms' advertisements, a sheaf of photocopies of Lynne's curriculum vitae, the few thanks-all-the-same notes in reply to her many letters, a list of the names and addresses of the firms she had written to. One of the names was Africa Hinterland. The address rang a bell in a detective's mind. It was of a suite of offices in the commercial complex at Greenwich where Scott Singleton had run a motor-repair shop. The perceptive detective drove to Greenwich, only three miles north of Catford, and learned that Africa Hinterland had ceased trading a week or so earlier than Singleton had. He saw, at the entrance to the complex, a row of pigeon-holes for the respective occupiers' mail – and was told that postmen had continued to stuff mail in Africa Hinterland's pigeon-hole for some time after the firm went bust. There was no way of proving that Lynne Rogers's letter was among the inopportune mail, let alone that Singleton filched it in passing – but still, it seemed to the investigators that here was another circumstance that went towards justifying their suspicion of him.

When Singleton was brought in for questioning at Crawley police station on 29 September, he complained that he was being 'harassed,' and said that he had been 'picked on simply because I've got a blue car and live in Crawley.'

He was tight-lipped in more ways than one. As well as being careful about what he said, he was careful about how he said it, never opening his mouth wider than a slit. Some newspaper reports of the discovery of Lynne Rogers's body had referred to the bite-mark on the chin, but none had revealed that the mark, promptly photographed by a scenes of crime officer, had been made by someone who was missing the right-centre incisor at the top and whose existing front teeth were malformed. During the questioning of Singleton, a detective carefully and casually asked him if he would allow an impression of his teeth to be taken. He shook his head.

On 1 October, after Michael Bennison, the detective superintendent leading the murder hunt, had conferred with solicitors of the Crown Prosecution Service, Singleton was released. But from the minute he left the station, he was kept under surveillance. There is no reason to believe that the officers given the watching brief were not ordered to act inconspicuously, avoiding the tiniest risk of making Singleton feel pressurized.

A number of lucky chances led to the solution of the case. One of the investigators happened to meet a Crawley policeman who happened to mention that, about a year before, when Singleton was suspected of a crime, he, the policeman, had searched the house in Wilkinson Court – and while doing so, without result, had happened to tread on a single-tooth dental plate, smashing it into smithereens. Yes, it was certainly Singleton's: his near-hysterical reaction had made that clear. As soon as the policeman's little tale was repeated to Superintendent Bennison, he instituted a search – fanning out from the neighbourhood of Wilkinson Court – for Singleton's dentist. When traced, the dentist produced Singleton's patient-card, which showed that he had last visited the surgery for a replacement of the broken dental plate. The dentist raised the detectives' hopes by saying that he had taken a plaster-cast of all

Singleton's teeth – and instantly dashed those hopes by adding that he didn't bother to keep old casts. As the disappointed detectives were leaving, a nurse who had heard part of their conversation with the dentist called them back. She was holding a small cardboard box labelled 'André Paul Reich,' Singleton's former name. It contained the cast of his teeth. She explained: 'Because he was such an awkward customer, I decided to keep it in case he came back and complained.' A forensic odontologist superimposed the impressions of the cast upon a photograph of the bite-mark, and concluded from the matching unusual configuration that there was no reasonable possibility that the bite-mark was not made by Singleton (at a time when he was not wearing his dental plate).

On 10 October, Singleton was arrested and charged with murder.

Between then and the trial, the police learned that he had subscribed to two dating services. Several women subscribers to one of the services claimed that he had accosted them, making improper advances, and when they had hurried away, had followed and loitered outside their homes or workplaces. One woman said that she had agreed to get into his car when he curb-crawled beside her, speaking to her by name and mentioning personal details about her. Belatedly made apprehensive by the strangeness of some of his comments, she had told him to stop the car, but he had driven to Wilkinson Court and tried to force her into the house, letting her go only because he was unable to gag her screams.

It is unclear where the police found a collection of flashlit snapshots of Singleton, for each of which he had adopted a different immodest pose and in all of which he was wearing female undergarments.

The evidences of his extreme and unconventional efforts to obtain sexual pleasures were viewed by Superintendent Bennison as confirmations of his belief, his certainty, that Singleton had thought that he only needed to lure Lynne Rogers into his car, and she, desperate to get the job he had talked about, would do anything he asked; when things had not gone to plan, he had seen no alternative but to silence her.

Till the trial, at Lewes Crown Court in July 1992, Singleton's lady-friend, the thrice-blessed Kim Arnold of Catford, remained steadfast; she had every intention of speaking up for him from the witness-box. But soon after the start of the trial, something caused her to turn against him. Not merely withdrawing her support, she changed sides, from the defence to the prosecution – to testify that, while looking among music cassettes at her home, she had come across an unmusical one, a recording of Singleton pretending to be an air-traffic-controller. The recording – which had circuitously become a trial exhibit, for it had been given to the police, not by Ms Arnold, but by the tabloid paper to which she had donated it – was played to the jury of six men and six women, some of whom meanwhile glanced at Suzanne Rogers, who, sitting with her father near the dock, was clearly affected by the sounds.

No doubt there was a sensible reason why the jury took more than four hours to decide that the defendant was guilty. The judge seems to have made a non-sequitur in his comments to Singleton before passing sentence: having said, 'I remain, as the jury must, ignorant of what actually happened after you took that girl into your custody,' he went on: 'That is a matter which gives me grave concern as to your dangerousness.'

The moment Mr Justice Alliott stopped speaking, Derek Rogers, no longer able to contain himself, lunged at the dock, shouting at Singleton: 'I will kill you! I will get you one way or the other – don't worry, I will!' Singleton, who had instantly retreated to the rear of the dock, his sleepy eyes suddenly widened by fear, was taken away by prison officers. Derek Rogers, now surrounded by policemen, shouted at the judge: '"Life" – is that all? After what he's done to my daughter, to my family, you put him away for only about twenty years.' The judge had by now left the bench. Derek Rogers held out his hands to his surviving daughter. She too was weeping. 'I'm sorry,' he said, 'I'm sorry.' But nobody could have blamed him.

The Fatal Homecoming

JUST AFTER LUNCHTIME on Sunday, 8 September 1991, thirty-year-old Catherine Gore, a laboratory manager, drove to her parents' home, a large cottage made from two small ones, in Chavenage Lane, on the edge of the Gloucestershire town of Tetbury. She meant to spend the afternoon with her parents. Her father, John Gore, was fifty-seven; the high dome of his head had been bald for many years, but the hair at the sides, always carefully brushed, was as extremely dark as it had always been, with no trace of grey. A doctor of science, he was the radiological protection manager at the Berkeley Nuclear Power Station in Gloucester, where he was known as 'a real gentleman, quietly-spoken, and very kind and considerate'. His wife Ruth, who was two years younger, ran a small catering business, and, to add to her several interests and pastimes, had recently acquired, and become fascinated with, a personal computer.

Catherine smelt smoke as soon as she unlocked the front door; saw flames when, already calling to her parents, she opened the door to the living-room. The flames, none of much size, were licking a mess of materials banked against the electric fire, which was fully on, and darting from the hearth-rug. The draught caused by the sudden opening of the door had sent bits of charred newspaper fluttering from the burning materials. As well as the smell of smoke, there was the smell of paraffin.

She may not have noticed that at the time – nor that, dreadfully incongruous, a felling-axe and a kitchen-knife lay beside a chintz-covered armchair that faced the television set. She managed to kick up the switch of the electric fire, and then rushed towards the kitchen. She had not stopped calling out to her parents. She continued to call out as, having reached the foot of the stairs, she mounted a couple of the steps, high enough for her to view the whole of the landing in the low-ceilinged cottage – to see her parents lying there, her father in pyjamas, her mother in a nightdress, both hacked to death. She staggered down the steps and on into the kitchen, where there was a phone.

The emergency services were soon at the cottage: firemen, who quickly doused the flames, ambulancemen, who after speaking to Catherine drove away, and policemen – uniformed constables at first, and then also detectives and scenes of crime officers; a police surgeon too.

The surgeon estimated that the murders had occurred in the early hours of the morning, probably soon after daybreak. The blood-drenched top pillow on John Gore's bed indicated that the killer, carrying the axe (brought from the garage) and with the kitchen-knife in a pocket or tucked inside a waistband, had crept into the room and arced the axe down into the sleeping man's skull; had done so again and again. The absence of blood in Ruth Gore's bedroom, across the landing, indicated that she, awoken by the noises, had entered her husband's room and been felled with a blow from the axe; if not already dead, further blows had killed her. Either between blows with the axe or afterwards, the killer had repeatedly stabbed the bodies with the kitchen-knife. For some reason, a seemingly unaccountable one, the killer had dragged the bodies on to the landing. Blood had been partially wiped from some surfaces – no doubt because the killer had left fingerprints in the blood – and the handles of the axe and the knife had been scoured: perhaps with a swab, unburnt bits of which were found on the hearth of the electric fire in the living-room.

The fire was equipped with a gadget for automatically igniting it at a pre-set time. It seemed that the killer had had two purposes in mind in banking materials around the fire, saturating them with paraffin (also with white spirit, subsequent analysis showed), and setting the gadget: to destroy both the building and incriminating evidence such as garments worn while committing the murders – remnants of a jazzily-patterned shirt and a pair of denim trousers, parts of them bloodstained, were picked from among the debris. The killer must have changed into other clothes, either brought to the house or found in it.

There were no banknotes in John Gore's wallet, nor in his wife's handbag. Either the bed in a guest-room had been used during the previous night or (most unlikely, according to a local woman who came in once or twice a week to help Mrs Gore with the cleaning) it had been used before then and not been re-made. The home-help also said that she thought some bottles of wine, including one of champagne, were missing. A search of the garbage awaiting collection revealed only one empty wine bottle. It was at the top of a bin, which suggested that it had been placed there very recently, and had been wiped free of fingerprints, which suggested, but more strongly, that it had been placed there by the killer. An upturned glass, thoroughly washed, stood alone on the draining-board in the kitchen, a fact that, put with the suggestions regarding the bottle, made it virtually certain that the killer had drunk wine after his labours.

When Catherine Gore was asked about close relatives whom she wished the police to inform of the tragedy, a look of a new sort of horror crossed her face. Foreboding mingled with that horror. Then she said that she had a brother, slightly younger than herself, Christopher. She had not seen him for quite a time, she couldn't be sure how long. She didn't know his address, but believed that he was living in Bath, where he had been at university.

A request for help in tracing Christopher Gore was sent to the police at Bath, which lies to the south-west of Tetbury, a distance of twenty miles as the crow flies. He was not listed in the telephone directory; his name was not entered on the electoral roll. Getting assistance from the university on a Sunday during a vacation required patience, but eventually someone said that Gore, C., had studied pure mathematics, and, again eventually, someone else divulged the names and home phone numbers of members of the mathematics department – one of whom remembered Christopher Gore as a brilliant student . . . but also as 'an extraordinarily disturbed young man'. He gained a first-class honours Ph.D., but would certainly have passed the examination far earlier than he did had there not been long breaks in his studies, the longest starting a few months after his arrival, when he wantonly destroyed equipment in a computer room and tore up banknotes, actions which resulted in his being sent to a psychiatric clinic. Soon after returning to the university he attempted suicide. Subsequently, while undergoing psychotherapy, he exhibited homicidal tendencies, particularly towards a nurse. He often spoke bitterly of his parents, blaming them for his mental disorder because, so he said, they starved him of affection and – his father especially – had over-high expectations of him.

Another lecturer who was phoned confirmed at least some of those facts, and said that, during the past couple of summers, he had often seen Christopher Gore doing a juggling act, its finale being with flaming torches, on the buskers' pitches in tourist-crammed parts of the city – outside the Roman baths and the medieval abbey, for instance.

A quizzing of street entertainers led the Bath police to the homes, most of them 'squats', of persons who were friendly with Christopher Gore, and it became clear that, from mid-afternoon, he had done a variation on a pub-crawl, starting with a carrier-bag filled with bottles of wine, sharing a bottle or two with one lot of friends, then with another lot, and so forth, till the bag was empty; he had split a bottle of vintage champagne with one lot of friends. The last lot said that they hadn't the faintest idea where he might have gone after leaving them.

Following the final phone-call of the night from the Bath police headquarters to the station at Tetbury, a police bulletin, specially carefully worded with regard to the search for the son of the murdered couple, was distributed among the news media. Next morning, it was quoted in reports of the crime contained in local television and radio programmes.

At about 10 a.m., a bearded or long-unshaven young man, dressed in a many-coloured shirt and torn jeans, entered a police station in Bath. He was balding, but his dark hair was long at the back and fashioned into a pigtail. 'My name is Christopher Gore,' he said. 'I believe you want me for two deaths and a fire.'

He was questioned – at first, briefly, by Bath detectives, and then, in fourteen sessions, by members of the Gloucestershire team of investigators, led by Superintendent Malcolm Hart. He insisted that he was innocent. Always as polite to the questioners as they were to him, he seemed actually to enjoy himself; before he sat down at the start of each of the early sessions, it was as if he were looking forward to a test that he was confident of passing, that would prove just how clever he was, and none of those sessions was ended at his wish: he was always keen to continue.

But meanwhile the police were gathering evidence against him, some of which not even he could reject on the grounds that it was based on faulty logic or arithmetical sophistry. Superintendent Hart's belief that Gore began 'to think of the questioning as a game' is supported by a comment made by Gore during one of the later sessions: 'You might have me in check, but it is not checkmate yet.' Whether or not, he was charged with the murders, and remanded in custody at Horfield Prison, Bristol.

Among the points of the police case was the evidence of a Tetbury cab-driver who, responding to a phone call at about noon on the Sunday, had picked up a man from a place near Chavenage Lane and driven him to the railway station at Chippenham, a dozen miles to the south. 'The way he was dressed looked a bit odd – shorts and a Bermuda-type shirt. He never said much. He didn't appear agitated at all.' The driver identified Gore as the man.

Several persons who had travelled to Bath on a train that left Chippenham station shortly after the cab's arrival there identified Gore as a fellow-passenger. He had spent most of the journey playing with two clockwork toys, a monkey and a ladybird. The toys had till lately stood among knick-knacks on a shelf in his mother's bedroom.

The killer of John and Ruth Gore had erased finger-print evidence but, perhaps when leaving, had noticed a newspaper sticking through the letter-box, and perhaps thinking that a local person passing by might see it, wonder why it had not been taken in, and check that all was well with the Gores, had pulled the newspaper through. In so doing, he had made fingerprints on the newspaper. They were Christopher Gore's.

Nine days after he was charged, he summoned Super-intendent Hart to the prison and admitted that he had murdered his parents. Showing no emotion, and saying nothing that could be construed as remorse, he clarified uncertainties in the 'crime scenario' that the investigators had pieced together: he had travelled to his parents' home on the Saturday, arriving there in the early evening . . . had dined with them . . . having stayed up for an hour or so after they had said goodnight, he had lain 'brooding' on the bed in the spare room – till about six in the morning, when he had gone to the garage for the axe and, 'after executing a few practice blows with it,' returned through the kitchen, where he had selected a knife, and walked upstairs and along the landing to his father's room . . . For part of the time before he left, he had sat in the living-room watching a video of a movie. (It would be interesting to know which movie it was, and whether he enjoyed it; but though his confession is said to have been 'pedantically exact,' he apparently omitted information on those small points.)

During the following year, he was examined by psychiatrists, who concluded that he had 'a remarkably abnormal schizoid personality' and that he harboured 'pathological hostilities, mainly towards women'. Their belief that his condition had existed since childhood seems to have been wholly or partly based upon recollections of former class-mates of his at a Roman Catholic school in Cheshire, who said, among other things, that he had spent much of his spare time writing poems on the theme of parricide.

In October 1992, he appeared before a judge at Bristol Crown Court. He denied murder, but admitted manslaughter on the grounds of diminished responsibility, a plea that was accepted by the prosecution. He stared at the floor throughout the thirty-minute hearing, at the end of which the judge ordered that he be confined in the Broadmoor Institution for an indefinite period: 'You need treatment, and need to be kept under restraint for a long time ahead.'

He was still settling in at Broadmoor when he was visited by West Country detectives who hoped that he might be able and willing to assist them with their inquiries into two unsolved murders, the first in June 1984 at Bath, the second in November 1989 in the village of Rodborough, near Stroud, ten miles from Tetbury.

One reason for the detectives' belief that he could help if he so desired was that he allegedly made a remark to a policeman before one of the interviews regarding the murder of his parents: 'I have committed two major crimes in your area, and you will never get me for them.'

The case in Bath was of the murder of Melanie Road, a seventeen-year-old sixth-former at the city's High School, whose body was found in a blind-alley near her home; she was the victim of what a police spokesman described as 'a frenzied attack, perhaps sexually motivated'.

The case in Rodborough was of the murder of Carmel

Gamble, a forty-three-year-old down-and-out, weighing only about seventy pounds, who was known in the area as 'the clog lady' because, whatever the weather and the time of year, she traipsed around in backless wooden shoes, barely visible beneath a coat discarded by a woman considerably taller than she was. Her body was found in her tiny cottage. She had been bludgeoned to death, probably with a hammer, and slashed with a pointed knife. The murderer had attached an electrical timer to a heater and surrounded it with combustible materials, with the intention, unfulfilled, of starting a fire. The police received an anonymous letter saying that the murderer had 'links' with Bath University and the Berkeley Nuclear Power Station. In a programme of the 'Crimewatch' series on BBC Television, Carmel Gamble's last known movements were reconstructed, and the head of the investigation showed artists' impressions of men seen with her in the days before her death. Following the arrest of Christopher Gore, Superintendent Hart and his subordinates noted that he strongly resembled the drawing of one of the men. And they were intrigued by the fact that newspaper cuttings relating to the murder of Carmel Gamble had been found scattered on the top of the television set at his parents' home.

The detectives who visited him in Broadmoor were unable to persuade him to talk about the unsolved murders. They intend to visit him again – if necessary, often. It is possible that he, so brilliant at reasoning, will, one of those days, take pity on them and suggest avenues of inquiry leading to solutions.

A Body in a
Bathroom

I HAVE NO IDEA how many people have died in the bath in the three-quarters of a century since the celebrated Brides-in-the-Bath case, but it is safe to say many thousands. And it is just as safe to say that more of those deaths than the few, the very few, that were not taken for granted as being either accidental or natural, liable to have happened in the bath or elsewhere, were murders – murders of the only truly perfect kind, those that raise no suspicion that murder has been done.

If Anthony Fraser had murdered simply, and solely with the aid of a bath, he might well have escaped prosecution. Despite the hash he made of the task, it seemed possible at one time that he would escape punishment.

Shortly before 6 p.m. on Saturday, 22 June 1991, he phoned for an ambulance to come to the maisonette in Wills Street, in the Lozells suburb of Birmingham, where he had lived for the past few years with his girlfriend, a spinster named Mary Weekes, who was thirty-two, five years younger than himself. It is reported that *she* had two young children, which indicates that she had had them by a man or men other than Fraser; I cannot tell where the children were that Saturday afternoon, but they were subsequently taken into care by the social services.

Fraser opened the door to the ambulance men and led them to the bathroom. Mary Weekes was lying naked, apparently dead, beside the bath. The floor around was puddled with water. It is understandable that the ambulance men did not notice whether or not any of the

58

upper parts of the body were damp, for their attention was concentrated on the dreadful swelling and blistering of almost all of the skin, clearly caused by immersion in scalding-hot water. Fraser was talking – saying, among other things, that he had gone out at half-past four after, at Mary's request, running a bath for her; he had returned and found her lying in the bath, had managed to pull her out, at the same time emptying the water, and had then dialled 999. As a matter of routine, one of the ambulance men felt for a pulse at the woman's neck . . . then he shouted to his colleague that she was not dead and applied artificial respiration.

Those were bad moments for Fraser. It had not occurred to him that he had failed to kill Mary Weekes. Was it possible that she could be revived – that she would be able to speak, to say what he had done?

She was taken to the city's Accident Hospital. She was still alive late that night, when detectives, having interviewed the ambulance men and visited the maisonette, took a preliminary statement from Fraser. She died, without having regained consciousness, at six o'clock on Sunday morning.

A post-mortem examination was carried out by an experienced forensic pathologist, Dr Helen Whitwell, who found that the scalding was not the only form of injury. Once the hair was shaved from the head, a dozen wounds were revealed; some had been inflicted with such force that the brain was injured. On the throat, partly obscured by the blistering, were bruises that were characteristic of manual strangulation. Dr Whitwell was sure that the attack had continued after the woman was deeply unconscious – therefore, on the strong assumption that the attack took place before her immersion in the bath, rather than during it, she must have been placed in the bath. A test for the presence of semen proved negative.

The detectives assigned to the case had a reason that was not associated with it for believing that Fraser was the murderer; the reason will be made clear in due

59

course. If he was innocent, the crime must have been committed within about half an hour from when he, having filled the bath (from the hot tap only), left his girlfriend alone – while the water was still at a scalding temperature. There was no sign of forced entry into the maisonette. It appeared that if Mary Weekes had opened the door to a caller, she had been naked, for no covering garment was lying in the area between the door and the bathroom. The police, as well as making house-to-house inquiries in and around Wills Street, set up a telephone 'hot line' for information, which could be given confidentially, but no one spoke of having seen a caller entering or leaving the maisonette during the latter part of Saturday afternoon.

However, a near-neighbour recalled seeing Fraser hurrying away, 'looking distressed', at around five o'clock, some thirty minutes after the time he said he had gone out. His statements were in several respects contradictory of things he had said to the ambulance men, and there were contradictions between the statements. He did not waver from his story that he had gone out to shop for a refrigerator, but was so determined to stick to it that he told reckless lies: for instance, his assertion that he had not had a drink while he was out was proved untrue by clear evidence that he had spent some time drinking in a pub. There seems no reason, other than that he suspected that he had been asked a trick-question, why he should have lied about the position of Mary Weekes's body in the bath when he returned home; but according to medical experts, his description did not tally with the different degrees of scalding on different parts of the body. The experts prepared a video illustrating the grounds for their opinion.

It was shown during Fraser's trial for murder at Birmingham Crown Court in April 1992.

At the end of that trial, the jury failed to agree upon a verdict. In the absence of a more likely explanation as to why some members of the jury, at least three, firmly refused to find Fraser guilty of murder, one can only suppose that they had been misled (not by defence counsel, of course) into believing that circumstantial evidence is second-rate evidence. That belief has become widespread through the constant reiteration of versions of the line, 'the evidence was no more than circumstantial,' in movies, television and radio programmes, crime novels, magazine and newspaper articles. If any of the writers of such lines were asked to say what other sort of evidence there is, they would be stumped. The answer is: *direct* evidence – that of eye-witnesses. All *indirect* evidence, including statements made by the accused and the evidence of expert witnesses, is circumstantial. Since relatively few murders are committed in the presence of an innocent third party, there are even fewer trials for murder in which there is *any* uncircumstantial evidence. Perhaps the time has come for judges at trials for covert murder to be required to stress the stupidity of disregarding circumstantial evidence simply because it *is* circumstantial.

If the jury at Fraser's re-trial in October 1992, also at Birmingham Crown Court, had failed to agree, the prosecution might have decided not to try again. But every member of that jury was sensible – unknowingly in accord with the view of the great American writer, Henry Thoreau, that 'some circumstantial evidence is very strong, as when you find a trout in the milk'. They needed only a couple of hours to decide that Fraser was guilty as charged.

The announcement of the verdict provoked cries – mostly of relief, one gathers – from two groups of people in the public gallery: relatives and friends of Mary Weekes, and relatives and friends of another dead woman. The judge, Mr Justice Popplewell, sentenced Fraser to life imprisonment, saying that he would recommend to the Home Office that 'life' should mean at least fifteen years.

The recommendation would not have been influenced by the fact – kept secret from the murder-case juries, of course – that in 1986, in the same court, Fraser had been acquitted of the manslaughter of Mrs Verlyn Herbert, his common-law wife, who had somehow been caused to fall down a flight of stairs with such force that she was knocked unconscious, and had died from choking on her vomit.

Beverley Allitt

The Killer Nurse on Ward 4

BRIAN MARRINER

WHILE THE PUBLIC OUTRAGE at the crimes of Beverley Allitt is understandable, it seems way over the top, with an hysterical undertone to it all. One would imagine that the most horrible and unnatural thing had taken place; that the moon had suddenly turned blue or that the sun had come out at midnight.

I am reminded of passages in the *Anglo-Saxon Chronicles*, penned by unknown monks a few hundred years after Christ. For the year AD 671, the entry reads: 'In this year was the great mortality of birds.' AD 685 was another bad year, the *Chronicles* recording: 'In this year there occurred in Britain bloody rain, and milk and butter were turned to blood.'

Well, if in 1993 our milk and rain have not turned to blood, then the pages of our more sensational tabloid newspapers have been more than usually gory, with such emotive terms as 'Angel of Death', and headlines reading: 'Worse Than Myra Hindley'. The plain fact is that we should not be amazed and surprised that members of the medical profession should kill their patients. There is a long history of them doing precisely that.

Beverley Allitt is by no means the first killer nurse. In Vienna an entire *team* of nurses were busy killing elderly patients between 1983 and 1988, injecting some of their 49 victims with insulin, and drowning others with a water-soaked face-cloth over the mouth and nose. Waltraud Wagner and Irene Leidolf were sentenced to life; two colleagues were sentenced for attempted murder. In 1986, in Wuppertal, West Germany, a nurse known as the 'Angel of Death' murdered 17 of her patients. Richard Angelo, a 27-year-old nurse was convicted in Long Island in 1987 of the murder of four patients by lethal injections. Donald Harvey, another male nurse, confessed to killing 30 elderly people over a period of years in Cincinnati, Ohio. He also confessed to killing his room-mate's father. Gwendolyn Graham was convicted of killing five women at the hospital where she worked in Grand Rapids, Michigan, in 1987. Joseph Atkin was investigated over the deaths of 15 patients in Birmingham, Alabama, and Atlanta, in 1992, and eventually was charged with the murder of one man by lethal injection. Brian Rosenfeld pleaded guilty to three murders in Largo, Florida, in 1992; up to 203 patients had died in his care. In a Toronto hospital, a number of unexplained deaths over a nine-month period led to the arrest of a nurse on the night-shift; a judge found that the deaths were not accidental or from natural causes, but the prosecution was dropped because there was equal suspicion against another nurse on the same shift. A sudden increase in cardiac arrests in the Ann Arbor Veterans Administrations Hospital in 1975 led to suspicions being aroused; investigation showed that a paralysing drug had been administered in three cases, but the culprit was never found. At a hospital in Nevada, a nurse on a murder charge was acquitted of tampering with a patient's life-support system. There were rumours that nurses had been running a sweepstake on when patients would die.

The most infamous case of a nurse turning killer happened in the US in 1982: Texan nurse Genene Jones, forty-one, a mother-of-two, was jailed for a total of 159 years for poisoning two children at the Bexar County Medical Centre in San Antonio where she worked. Jones was also suspected of murdering 23 other babies at

Bexar. The paperback book on the case, *The Death Shift*, by Peter Elkind, was published in Britain in 1990, the year before Allitt's murders, and there are astonishing similarities between the two women. Both were chubby, overweight women who worried about their health. Both satisfied an obsessive craving for attention by injecting the children in their care with lethal drugs. We shall never know if Allitt read the book, but certainly she spent hours in the hospital library reading up on drugs and their properties.

Nor is Beverley Allitt the first to kill with insulin – that dubious distinction belongs to English male nurse Kenneth Barlow, who murdered his wife, Elizabeth, with a massive injection of insulin in 1957.

We may even consider ourselves fortunate that we have not experienced many more such deaths. Last year (1992), a bogus GP was jailed at Leeds Crown Court. His prescriptions over the years had included shampoo to be taken internally, and creosote for a tooth complaint. Yet he had practised undetected for thirty years. Only the vigilance of the chemist who dispensed his prescriptions prevented tragic consequences.

Another bogus hospital doctor was detected only after a patient died. He was not uncovered earlier, despite his habit of wandering around the hospital in a green operating-theatre uniform. *The hospital had no operating theatre* . . .

Yet the public alarm is understandable. We tend to trust nurses, to believe that when we go into hospital we are going to be treated, have our wounds healed, be guarded night and day against the sudden onset of heart failure or other evils. Not for nothing is nursing known as the 'caring profession', even if nurses are not, as they are so often described, 'angels'. They are ordinary people who have been trained to perform certain basic medical procedures. There is mounting pressure for nurses to be allowed to prescribe drugs, so releasing doctors for more important work. The Allitt case may well put an end to that initiative, which would be a pity.

An experienced nurse is the equal of a newly-qualified doctor in many areas.

Instead of blindly condemning Allitt and calling for the return of hanging, we should try to understand exactly what happened, why such a monstrous thing occurred, and what can be done to prevent a repetition. The first thing to take on board is the recognition that certain professions attract certain types. It is well-known, for example, that the job of prison officer attracts some sadistic men who long for power over others, and for this reason prison officers have to undergo psychological screening designed to weed out such types in the training period.

The police force attracts the same basic type, and the fire service has recruited men who actually became arsonists in order to have fires to put out so they could be portrayed in a heroic light. Paedophiles are attracted to jobs which bring them into contact with children, such as teaching and various social service occupations. Homosexuals may enlist in all-male branches of the armed forces. And many criminals have sought – and sometimes obtained – jobs as security guards. The foxes guarding the chickens . . .

Before even discussing the question of evil, it is necessary to recognize that Beverley Allitt was afflicted by a rare psychological condition called the Munchausen Syndrome. Doctors recognized long ago that certain patients become 'addicted' to hospitals, sometimes deliberately injuring themselves so as to be admitted. There are surgery freaks who swallow spoons and the like so that they can be operated on – some have so many abdominal scars that surgeons are unable to find anywhere to cut. In the main, people suffering from this condition (although suffering is the wrong word, since they enjoy it) have very low self-esteem and crave attention. Cutting their own wrists seems a price worth paying to become the centre of attention.

When doctors recognized this, they could hardly put 'malingering' on a patient's record for fear that the patient might see it. Instead, they chose Munchausen's Syndrome, because in the fable, Baron Munchausen was given to incredible, spectacular lies.

It was only in 1977 that a variation on this, Munchausen's Syndrome by Proxy, was diagnosed by Roy Meadows, a professor of paediatrics in Leeds. People with Munchausen's Syndrome harmed only themselves when they went to hospitals with fabricated illnesses. Professor Meadows drew attention to mothers who, instead of injuring themselves, injured their children in order to gain medical attention. It was invariably the mother who made her child sick by administering salt to make them vomit, or laxatives to induce diarrhoea, or even adding blood to urine samples or rubbing irritant substances on the child's skin. Even cases of cot death are sometimes caused by mothers who went too far to induce illness by depriving the child of oxygen.

It seems incredible that a devoted mother should deliberately harm her child and lie to hospital staff, but it happens all too often. Just as the notion of child sex-abuse by parents was hard to swallow at first, so this recently-recognized condition will only gradually come to be accepted – as a result of the Allitt case. Fortunately it is an extremely rare condition, but what we have learned is that persons with this complaint often have a history of an abused or loveless childhood, have an abnormal personality, and have a knowledge of medicine. Many of them join a caring profession as an expression of unmet needs to be loved, to be the centre of attention. But what must be stressed is that a woman suffering from this condition is not insane. She goes about deceiving others with a breathtaking cunning, inventing such complex fabrications that she fools even the experts. Her deadly work is done in such a clandestine fashion that she may even be capable of deceiving herself, refusing to accept that she is responsible for the harm she has caused. However, this was not the case with Allitt. She knew full well what she was doing, taking elaborate pains to conceal the evidence of her crimes to avoid detection. She made the *choice* to kill – not once, but several times.

It all began when Beverley Allitt decided she wanted to become a nurse. Or did it? It is often impossible to pinpoint the precise moment at which an individual goes wrong. Beverley Allitt, born 4 October 1968 in the village of Corby Glen, ten miles from Grantham in Lincolnshire, appeared to be a normal child with a love of other children. She was always in demand for babysitting. However, school friends remember that she often appeared at school with bandages around her head and told fantastic stories of how she had come by her injuries. Failing her 11-plus, she left school at sixteen and began a two-year pre-nursing course at Grantham College. Weighing thirteen stone, she was a little too masculine for some tastes, and hated being called 'Big Bev'.

She had boyfriends, but her relationship with them was far from normal. She used to beat them up quite badly, and one to whom she became engaged came to the conclusion that she was a lesbian. Later events indicated that he was probably correct.

In September 1988 she was accepted by Grantham and Kesteven District Hospital for training as a state-enrolled nurse. The hospital is a sprawling warren of Victorian buildings and concrete blocks, set in well-tended grounds. Allitt lived in nurses' quarters. By the autumn of 1989, at the end of her first year of training, there were already disturbing signs of her personality disorder. Strange things were going on in the nurses' quarters. Keys went missing and some nasty practical joker smeared human faeces on door-handles and put excreta under the kitchen cooker-grill. The police were eventually called in, but the culprit was never detected. Allitt was one of four suspects. She had spent two months in the geriatric ward and disliked it. She told a boyfriend that some of the patients were so old and feeble that the doctors secretly 'put them to sleep' with heroin overdoses. This was untrue, of course, but perhaps it was a clue to her thinking pattern.

Allitt was an average trainee nurse, working on all the wards at Grantham, and was popular with her fellow students. But her training was suffering because of her health problems. She was proving to be something of a hypochondriac. In her training years, she made over fifty visits to the hospital's casualty department and to doctors at other hospitals, complaining of a variety of ailments, most of which appeared to have been self-inflicted. Consider the record:

30 September 1985 Injury caused by kicking door. X-ray on little toe.

24 February 1986 Injury to right middle finger.

October Three visits to complain of abdominal pains. Admitted to hospital as a patient, telling nurses she had two ulcers. She said she had been vomiting, producing bowls of green vomit. The staff concluded that she was making herself sick.

December Crush injury to right hand, said to have been caused by squash racket.

December Gall bladder investigation following complaints of pain. The surgeon wrote on her case-notes: 'My feeling is that the symptoms are psychosomatic, reflecting stress in her family circumstances.'

30 March 1987 Complained of difficulty in moving hand.

5 May Physiotherapist noted a puzzling pattern. 'At end of session her hand is moving freely, but three days later she is back with a stiff hand.'

4 June Swollen right hand.

10 June Bruise to right hand; said she had fallen off bike.

13 November Said she had trapped thumb in car door, but doctor suspected that the injury was self-inflicted.

7 July 1988 Possible fracture of wrist; nothing found.

September Complained of straining back muscle

while lifting patient. Returned three days later with same complaint.

20 January 1989 Complained of head injury and double vision following a fall.

2 February Complained of two-day headache after the head injury.

25 February Headache after same fall.

14 March Referred for possible surgery for back strain; complained of blurred vision and headaches.

March Symptoms of urinary infection. Reported blood in her urine, but none seen by doctors.

8 August Injury to right foot.

October Minor injury to left leg.

14 January 1990 Complained of injury to right hand.

May Urine retention. Hospital admission for five days.

July Complained of severe colic pains; seen by urology specialist at Nottingham City Hospital, who noted 'hysterical symptoms'.

17 August Injury to right ankle.

3 October Complained of stomach pains. Laparoscope examination of abdomen, viscera, uterus. Had complained of blood in urine. Examination found urine clear, nothing amiss. The surgical wound was later tampered with and became infected.

10 October Appendectomy wound was oozing and bleeding in a manner which suggested that Allitt had pulled stitches apart.

13 May 1991 Apparent urinary infection, but X-ray showed nothing amiss.

15 May Small cuts to left foot.

July Acute retention of urine, temperature up, scratch marks on abdomen. Doctor noted: 'A very strange lady. A temperature of 41 degrees does not generally fall to normal within 30 seconds. Guess that thermometer was warmed.'

July Three punctures found on right breast, which was swollen. Doctors suspected that she had injected liquid into her breast.

August Dr Srinivasen of Edith Cavell Hospital commented: 'I'm not sure whether we are dealing with a Munchausen.'

At one point Allitt complained of a brain tumour, but a scan showed nothing. At another point in this grotesque charade, a physiotherapist noted: 'This woman is not fit to be a nurse.'

Incredibly, nothing was ever done, no action ever taken on these warnings.

Between October 1988 and November 1990, Allitt had been off sick for a total of 160 days. In her last year alone she had had 94 days of sick-leave, which led to her qualification as a nurse being delayed. She had visited the hospital's casualty department more than twenty times before being accepted for training as a nurse in 1988 at the South Lincolnshire School of Nursing. Six months later she began her practical experience at Grantham hospital, where between October 1988 and November 1990 she worked on various wards, including No. 4, the children's ward. In those years she had again visited the casualty department many times with obvious self-inflicted injuries. Yet these clues were never picked up.

Because of all the time she had taken off, she was told that she had to work an extra ten weeks before being allowed to register as a state-enrolled nurse, despite having sat her 90-minute nursing exam in October 1990, passing with average marks. She began her extra ten weeks of training on Ward 4 at the start of December.

Allitt was the only trainee on her course not to be offered a job at Grantham. She did apply for a post at the hospital, but was rejected following a 'very unsatisfactory' interview. It was noted that she was the 'worst candidate' interviewed in years.

On 13 February 1991 Allitt was turned down for work

at another hospital, following another unsatisfactory interview. On 14 February she reported that the key to the insulin fridge on Ward 4 was missing. On 15 February she completed her training and had another interview for a job at Grantham.

She had been turned down for jobs on all the adult wards at Grantham, and now applied for training as a children's nurse but was again rejected. This time, however, she was listed as a 'first reserve' because of her previous experience and was offered a short-term contract as an enrolled nurse. The reason for this was that the children's ward was acutely understaffed. Sheer desperation had let a killer loose.

On Monday, 18 February 1991, Allitt began her six-month contract on Ward 4. She entered the professional nursing register on 19 February. Five days later, her first victim was dead . . .

It is significant that once Allitt was installed on Ward 4, her hypochondria ceased and her visits to casualty stopped. (They were to resume during her months on police bail following her arrest.) This was because she now ceased being a Munchausen and became instead a Munchausen *by Proxy*. She would prove her value, her qualities as a nurse, by heroically saving the lives of desperately ill children. Children she herself had made ill . . .

Now began the chilling 59 days of terror on Ward 4. Between 21 February and 22 April 1991, Allitt attacked thirteen children who were in her care.

Seven-week-old Liam Taylor was the first to die. He had been admitted to the hospital on 21 February because of a cold on his chest, but within hours of his admittance to Ward 4 he collapsed with respiratory arrest. Brought back to health and seemingly on the mend – the parents were told they could take him home within a couple of days – Allitt attacked him again on 23 February, causing cardiac arrest and death. The pathologist's report diagnosed an unexplained heart attack.

Consultants were baffled by the child's death, but it was to be ten weeks before a police investigation was launched, and in those ten weeks another twelve children were to suffer at Allitt's hand.

By the end of April, three more sick children had died and nine others had become critically ill. Some Allitt had injected with drugs; others she had simply suffocated. But throughout the ensuing turmoil, she was always in the thick of things as the super-nurse, unselfishly and devotedly caring for the children. It was always she who raised the alarm and assisted the emergency medical teams which attempted to resuscitate her victims. It was usually Allitt who reported that a child had 'gone a funny colour' or 'looked blue'. No one suspected that the 'angel' on Ward 4 was armed with syringes filled with lethal drug doses; that the angel had become a destroyer.

So good was Allitt's act that many parents developed a rapport with her, grateful to her for being a saviour. The parents of one victim were so grateful that they asked her to become godmother to the twin which survived.

It was almost two weeks before Allitt killed again. This time the victim was Timothy Hardwick, a severely disabled eleven-year-old who had been admitted on 5 March after suffering fits at school. Later that same day, another nurse noticed that he was barely breathing and had turned blue. An emergency team attempted resuscitation, but by 6.15 pm he was dead. The post-mortem found that he had died from epilepsy.

The mysterious collapses became more frequent, five children suffering unexplained attacks during March, and at least seven more during two weeks in April. Allitt was on duty during all these crises and revelled in the attention. The doctors were becoming frantic, unable to explain what was going on and suspecting everything from legionnaire's disease to bacterial contamination, drug contamination, and even the possibility that one of the nursing staff was an infection carrier. They checked

73

whether wrong treatments had been given. But no one suspected that Allitt was responsible.

She was the heroine, with colleagues praising her dedication. One said later: 'It sounds crazy now, but everyone used to feel sorry for Bev. She was always in the thick of things.'

Allitt made her own comment. When one child twice stopped breathing, she casually pointed out to other nurses that she had been present at a number of such incidents on the ward and added: 'Maybe it's a jinx.'

On 10 March she attacked Kayley Desmond, aged 15 months, causing two respiratory arrests. The child was transferred to another hospital, where she survived. On 13 March Allitt attacked Paul Crampton, aged 5 months, injecting him with insulin, causing hypoglycaemia. On 21 March she attacked him again, and on 28 March struck again with an insulin injection, causing another hypo and near-death. Paul was transferred to another hospital and survived. His blood was ordered to be sent for urgent tests for possible insulin, but missed the post and was stored until after the Easter holiday.

On 30 March Allitt attacked Brad Gibson, aged five, causing cardiac arrest. The child 'died' for 32 minutes. He was transferred to another hospital and survived, but with permanent damage.

On 31 March Allitt attacked Henry Chan, aged two, causing two respiratory arrests. The child was transferred to another hospital and survived. On 2 April Paul Crampton's 'urgent' blood sample finally left the hospital to be tested in Cardiff.

On 4 April Allitt attacked Becky Phillips, aged nine weeks, causing hypoglycaemia. The child had been admitted for an upset stomach; following her discharge from hospital, she suffered a series of convulsions, ending in her death at her parents' home. A pathologist diagnosed cot death. Paul Crampton's blood sample finally arrived at Cardiff, where it was stored in a fridge.

On 5 April Katie Phillips, Becky's twin, was admitted

to hospital for observation. Allitt attacked her within hours of her arrival on Ward 4, causing a respiratory arrest. On 7 April she attacked the child again, causing respiratory and cardiac arrest. Katie 'died' for 45 minutes, and was put on a life-support system. She was transferred to another hospital, where she survived, although permanently brain-damaged. An X-ray showed that she had five broken ribs, as if someone had shaken her roughly or crushed her. However, the child's mother, Susan, was so grateful to Allitt for noticing her child's deteriorating condition that she invited her into her home and asked her to become Katie's godmother – which Allitt graciously did.

On 9 April Allitt attacked Michael Davidson, aged seven, causing a brief cardiac arrest. The child survived. By now a doctor on Ward 4 had suggested the possibility that they had a Munchausen at work, since normally they would have expected perhaps one fatality per year, but his warning appears to have been ignored.

On 12 April Paul Crampton's blood was finally tested in Cardiff and was found to contain massive amounts of rejected insulin. Grantham Hospital was notified, and the doctors and junior manager agreed to keep close observation but to say nothing.

On 13 April Allitt attacked Chris Peasgood, aged eight weeks, causing respiratory arrest twice. The child was transferred to another hospital and survived. The following day Allitt attacked Christopher King, aged five weeks, causing a brief respiratory arrest. The child's mother, a nurse at the hospital, was not informed. The management wanted to keep their deadly secret to themselves for fear of panic.

On 16 April Allitt attacked Christopher King again, causing three suspected respiratory and cardiac arrests. The child was transferred to another hospital and survived. On 19 April Allitt attacked Patrick Elstone twice, causing respiratory arrest. The child was transferred to another hospital and survived, but with permanent damage.

On 22 April Allitt attacked Claire Peck, aged 15 months, on two occasions, causing cardiac arrest and death. Blood tests showed an abnormal level of potassium. The doctor in charge of Ward 4 raised the alarm, but, incredibly, no action was taken. However, doctors were becoming increasingly suspicious. 'It was one of the most terrible experiences of my career,' said one, talking about how Claire had suddenly stopped breathing for no apparent reason. 'I was very puzzled that we could not resuscitate this child.' On 26 April Dot Lowe, aged seventy-nine, suffered a severe hypoglycaemic attack in the old people's home where Allitt was moonlighting.

It was on 29 April that Professor David Hull, of Queen's Medical Centre, telephoned a Grantham doctor, urging him to inform the police. That same day, a mysterious fire broke out on Ward 4. On 30 April, following another telephone call from Professor Hull, hospital manager Martin Gibson finally bowed to pressure and called in the police.

It was a difficult investigation for the detectives, who knew nothing of medical matters and had to rely on what the doctors told them. What they did know from the start was that there had been a number of unexplained deaths and attacks on young children on Ward 4. Some had been injected with lethal drug doses, others appeared to have been suffocated. Only a nurse or doctor could have been responsible, and given the injections of potassium and insulin, a nurse seemed the likely bet.

At first Professor Hull believed that only three of the cases warranted investigation, but the police decided not to narrow the scope of their inquiry. In the first two weeks of May, detectives spent time reading medical journals, examining records, and questioning members of the staff. The obvious starting point was to find out which nurse had been on duty during all the attacks. The problem with that was that the ward log listing staff rotas was missing. It was an ordinary exercise book in which nurses signed in and were allocated to patients.

What led the police to Allitt was careful questioning

of other nurses. Some of them had seen things which hadn't appeared important at the time. And there was the fact that only Allitt had been on duty during each of the twenty-five collapses. Then came a telephone call from Dr Derrick Teale, a biochemist at St Lukes's Hospital, Guildford. The police had asked for additional tests on the blood samples, and Dr Teale was now able to state that Paul Crampton had been injected with the second-highest dose of insulin recorded in Great Britain: 43,147 milli-units of insulin for every litre of blood. A normal reading would have been between 12 to 15 milli-units. The only higher reading recorded was in the case of a doctor who committed suicide by injecting himself with insulin. Dr Teale's tests also revealed that Becky Phillips had been intentionally injected with insulin before her death.

Detective Superintendent Stuart Clifton, the Lincolnshire Police officer leading the investigation, finally interviewed Allitt on 21 May. She had no criminal record and appeared very cool and self-possessed, denying all knowledge of any attacks on patients.

'All those times I was on duty, do you think I would be so stupid to keep doing it?' she asked. Her relaxed manner was enough to alert the detective. An innocent person would have been flustered and even angry at the accusations.

When Allitt's flat in Grantham was searched, police found the missing ward log. Fifty-nine pages had been torn out. They covered the crucial days when the attacks had taken place, detailing which nurse had been allocated to which patient. Also found was an envelope on which was written the names and personal details of two of the victims.

When Superintendent Clifton formally charged Allitt with murder, she didn't bat an eyelid, but remained ice-cool. She persisted in denying everything. But a clue to her low self-esteem came when she told detectives: 'I am not competent – far from it. I am one of the bloodiest crappiest nurses out. I am the lowest of the low.' She never showed any remorse, and, kept at the police station overnight, slept so soundly that she had to be woken for a court appearance.

Eventually she was released on police bail and was given refuge by her best friend, fellow nurse Tracey Jobson, who took her into the family home in Peterborough, where she stayed for several weeks. But in that time strange things began to happen at the house. Bleach was poured on to carpets, bathroom curtains were scorched, money disappeared, and a knife was found plunged into a pillow. The family's dog was discovered coughing up tablets. Detective Superintendent Clifton confirmed after the case that 'a sequence of bizarre events took place at Peterborough, about forty in all.' Allitt remarked innocently that she thought a poltergeist was at work in the house – but she was the only evil spirit present there. Even now, awaiting trial for her life, she was up to her old tricks.

On 15 June she visited Katie Phillips at her home, having become great friends with her mother, who was convinced of her innocence and had even hired private detectives to try to prove it. But while Allitt was there, taking Katie out in her pram, the child suffered another respiratory attack.

Also in June, the lab tests on blood samples from the victims came in. An insulin expert had found massive amounts of that substance in various samples. A ward sister remembered that the key to the fridge where the insulin was stored had gone missing after she had sent Allitt to fetch some eye-drops.

On 14 August Jonathan Jobson, the fourteen-year-old son of the people she was staying with, suffered a hypoglycaemic attack. In September, Jean Saville, forty-nine, a night sister on Ward 4, committed suicide because of her guilt feelings at not having realized what had been happening. She became another of Allitt's victims.

On 21 November 1991 Allitt appeared at Grantham magistrates' court, charged with four murders and eight attempted murders. The van bringing her to court was besieged by angry women. For her own safety as much as anything else, Allitt was remanded in custody to New Hall women's prison at Wakefield. On four occasions she was rushed to nearby Pinderfields Hospital, suffering from self-inflicted injuries.

In February 1992 she again appeared at Grantham magistrates' court to be charged with three further attempted murders. By now she had developed anorexia nervosa. Doctors were baffled when she began vomiting regularly despite having eaten nothing. The mystery was solved when they realized that she had been swallowing her own faeces. In August she was transferred to Rampton secure hospital, having lost five stone in weight, placing her health in danger of permanent damage.

The next big event was to be the trial of Beverley Allitt. Here she would be granted all the attention she had ever wanted. The big question was whether the prosecution would be able to prove the charges against her. Allitt was very manipulative; she had managed to persuade a good many people of her innocence, including her own parents.

THE TRIAL

When she appeared at Nottingham Crown Court on Monday, 15 February 1993, she faced twenty-six counts in the indictment, including four of murder, eleven attempted murders, and eleven alternative counts of causing grievous bodily harm with intent. One of the murder charges related to the woman in the old people's home. Now aged twenty-four, she looked pale and haggard in the dock, flanked by two nurses. She wore no make-up, her hair was cropped short, and she was dressed in a shirt and trousers. She pleaded not guilty.

Mr John Goldring, QC, prosecuting, began his opening speech to the jury by telling them starkly that there had been a killer loose on Ward 4 at Grantham and Kesteven Hospital between February and April 1991. He told of the first murder, that of Liam Taylor, saying that the doctors had been puzzled why so young a child should have suffered a heart attack. As the number of children inexplicably collapsing had increased, the staff in charge of the ward had become increasingly worried. On 30 April they had called in the police.

The first death the detectives had examined was that of Paul Crampton, who had collapsed six times in three days in March. Tests had shown a huge amount of insulin in the baby's blood, and experts had concluded that a whole adult syringe of insulin had been injected into the child for no conceivable medical reason.

'The medical mystery was now over,' Mr Goldring continued. 'It was clear, incredible as it may seem, that there was a criminal at large on Ward 4. The person – the criminal – had to have access to a hypodermic syringe and had to know how to use it. The person – the criminal – had to have access to insulin. The task for the police was plain – they had to try and find the answer to the question: Who was that criminal on Ward 4?

'Detectives found that someone had cut out pages relating to Paul Crampton's stay in hospital from the ward notebook. Someone who didn't want the police to see what had taken place had cut out a number of pages. What did it mean? It meant that the criminal had access to that book and knew that each collapse in the ward was to be looked at afresh.' Later, a book which showed which nurse had been allocated to which patient vanished. It was found in a wardrobe at Allitt's home.

'What on earth was it doing there?' Mr Goldring asked rhetorically. 'Her explanation to the police was wholly unconvincing.' He went on to say that a chart indicating who was on duty in the ward was examined – and 'a chilling fact emerged. One has only to look at that document to see what the link was.' There was no suspicious collapse when Allitt was not on duty . . . Nurse Allitt had been present at each of the twenty-four attacks thought to have taken place on patients. The next nurse on the list was present ten times. . . We cannot say in each case exactly what the defendant did to a particular child. No one was watching her. Nurses are not expected to assault their patients. In some cases she injected insulin. In other cases, you may conclude, she injected or introduced through the baby's drip-feed a drug or strange mixture of drugs, which were readily available to her. In some she may simply have placed a hand over a baby's mouth or nose, interfering with the oxygen supply with dramatic consequences for a child who was ill. There were no witnesses, no one there to see what was done.'

Mr Goldring said of the many collapses on the ward: 'Nothing like it had happened before. Nothing like it has happened since. The epidemic ceased when Allitt was arrested.'

On the third day of the trial, the father of Liam Taylor went into the witness box. Fighting back tears, he told of how he and his wife were sleeping in a room at the hospital, just twenty feet away from where their son lay. They were woken at 5 am to be told that he had 'taken a turn for the worse'. Mr Taylor said: 'He had suffered a cardiac arrest and the doctors thought he had suffered severe brain damage because he had been deprived of oxygen.' Speaking of Allitt, he said: 'She was no different to the other nurses except she would give you the answer you would like to hear.'

A doctor admitted under cross-examination that he had mistakenly inserted an air-tube into Liam's food pipe instead of his windpipe, following his cardiac arrest, but denied that it had been left there for as long as twenty minutes, thus limiting his breathing. A senior physiotherapist who had treated Liam said that she was 'stunned' by the heart-attack: 'I did not expect him to have a cardiac arrest. It was bizarre.' Dr Charith Nanayakkara, the consultant paediatrician in charge of the children's ward, said that he was very surprised at

Liam's death, as he was generally very healthy and should have recovered. While the doctor was giving evidence, Liam's mother rushed weeping from the court, unable to bear the strain any longer.

A senior staff nurse testified that during her ten years on Ward 4, there had only been four or five children who had suffered cardiac or respiratory arrests – until Allitt arrived to work there. Then there had been a 'positive rash' of them.

Mr Goldring had said that nurses at Grantham Hospital had commiserated with Allitt because she was always on duty when children suddenly collapsed, yet she was never seen to show any emotion. Two nurses testified that when they asked Allitt if she was all right, fearing that she might be suffering from stress as a result of the many traumas, she shrugged off their concern, saying: 'I'm all right.'

Speaking of the heart-attack suffered by Brad Gibson, a doctor who worked at the hospital to which the child was transferred testified that he had concluded that the child had been injected with a drug by mistake. He told the court: 'Mistakes do occur and accidents do occur . . . Sometimes people are given the wrong drug, or the right drug in the wrong dose.'

Mrs Susan Phillips, mother of the murdered twin Becky and the damaged twin Katie, testified about her friendship with Allitt, saying: 'She seemed very competent and I trusted her.' Telling of how she had once left Katie's room for twenty minutes to telephone her parents, she said: 'When I left her, she was fine. When I came back, she was in a life-support machine. Apparently she had had a cardiac arrest – she looked as though she was dead.'

Mrs Phillips gave a harrowing account of the death of Becky, a few hours after the child's release from hospital: 'She was screaming pitifully. I have never heard a cry like it before, nor have I heard it since.'

It was immediately after this that the court was told that Allitt was unfit to attend any further hearings, since she was seriously ill with anorexia, having to be force-fed with a nasal tube. However, as Allitt had given her consent for the hearing to continue, the judge ruled that the trial would go on in her absence, defence counsel being allowed to visit her once a week in hospital to take instructions. The central figure in the case would be missing from the dock for the remainder of the proceedings. The web of evidence would be examined without the spider's presence.

Nurse Janet Sargeant wept as she testified about leaving Claire Peck alone on the treatment couch with Allitt while she went to speak to the baby's parents: 'When I got back to the room, Beverley said Claire had gone blue. She was not doing anything. Claire was on the couch. I rushed over to her and picked her up and turned her on her side.' She tried to give oxygen to the baby, who was 'blue around the lips and ears . . . her face was grey.' Mr Goldring asked her if Claire was breathing at this point. 'No,' she replied, 'but when I patted her, she started up again.' Asked what Allitt was doing, she replied: 'She was standing near the couch but she was not touching Claire. She did not do anything.' In other words, Allitt had made no attempt to resuscitate the child.

Afterwards, Allitt was again left alone with Claire, and the child suffered another respiratory failure. Student doctor Sangay Bhagani said in a statement that he was present in the treatment room when attempts were made to resuscitate Claire. 'Her heartbeat had stopped and everyone was working hard to resuscitate Claire, but her heart would not start again. Claire opened her eyes but we could not hold her. After working on Claire for about one and a half hours, the parents were brought to the treatment room and Claire was placed in her mother's arms, where she died almost straight away.' Dr Peter Lubke, A senior house-officer responsible for anaesthetics, said that he noted heart-rhythms in Claire consistent with potassium poisoning: 'I felt very sad and shocked. It was one of the most terrible experiences of my medical career. But, apart from that, I was very puzzled that we could not resuscitate this child.' Evidence was given that a post-mortem examination showed that the level of potassium in her blood was so high that it was off the scale of hospital equipment.

Claire's mother, Sue Peck, described Allitt's behaviour as she cradled her dying daughter: 'I just wanted some help. Everybody either looked away or looked at the floor, but Allitt just stood there. I will never, ever forget it. She was just staring, staring, staring at me.'

Nursing auxiliary Alice Stewart testified that, while on duty with Allitt at a nursing home in Leicestershire, she saw her give 79-year-old Dorothy Lowe an injection. Mrs Lowe had been ill during the night, so Mrs Stewart went into her room to see if she was all right. She told of what she saw.

'Bev Allitt was stood at the side of Dot's bed with her back towards the door and injecting into Dot's arm. I said she could have asked me and I would have helped her, but she made no reply and walked away.' The deputy matron at the nursing home told of finding Mrs Lowe 'in an unrousable state' the following morning.

On 25 March it was the turn of teenager Jonathan Jobson to testify. He told of how he had began suffering from dizzy spells shortly after Allitt came to live at his home; his condition had improved when he was away from home on work experience. He described how in August 1991 he was given a blackcurrant drink by Allitt, who was then on police bail: 'Bev asked me if I would like a drink. It didn't taste unusual, but halfway through I noticed a chalky powdery substance at the bottom of the glass. I remarked about the glass being dirty. I was quite annoyed that I had been given a dirty glass. She just replied that she had got the glass from the cupboard.' Afterwards, he had begun to feel nauseous. 'My headache just grew and grew, and suddenly the light faded and I could not see a thing. The next thing I knew, I was on the floor.' Of his sudden addiction to chocolate, he said: 'Basically I could not get enough. I was spending two or three pounds a day on chocolate, and if I could not get it, I became irritable.'

On 30 March the jury heard part of a tape-recording of a police interview with Allitt during which she claimed: 'I am telling the truth. God's honour, it is the truth.' When asked if she had injected Paul Crampton with insulin, she replied: 'I deny giving him anything other than the medication prescribed. I would not give anything maliciously . . . I am being accused of something I have not done and would not dream of doing.'

Detective Inspector Neil Jones told the court that when he asked Allitt to explain why she appeared to be 'a common denominator' – on duty when many of the incidents happened – she said flippantly: 'I don't know why. Is it something I am carrying?'

In late April it was the turn of the defence to call its witnesses. Professor Peter Berry, a paediatric pathologist, sought to cast doubts on the claim that children had been murdered on Ward 4. He told the court that in some cases he could not exclude criminal activity, such as the deliberate obstruction of breathing or the administering of a non-therapeutic substance, but he thought that other explanations were more likely. Professor Berry, an expert on sudden-infant-death syndrome, said that it was most likely that Liam Taylor had died from a respiratory tract infection; although other possibilities could not be excluded, he could find no clues from notes of the post-mortem to suggest otherwise. Timothy Hardwick was a deaf and blind epileptic with cerebral palsy, and children with such conditions could die unexpectedly from relatively trivial breathing infections. Becky Phillips could have died from a rare heart condition, and Claire Peck from acute asthma.

The defence had prepared a blackcurrant drink laced with the same tablets that Allitt was alleged to have used on Jonathan Jobson. This was passed around the jury, who were asked to note the surface scum left by the dissolving pills, obvious to anyone drinking it. A toxicologist, Dr Robyn Braithwaite, said that dissolving tablets in the drink would certainly leave tell-tale signs floating on top, but when cross-examined, he agreed that the scum could have been removed simply by flicking it off with a spoon.

On Thursday, 6 May, the leading defence counsel, James Hunt, QC, began his closing speech to the jury, asking them to imagine the 'nightmare' of being falsely accused of a catalogue of murders and attempted killings. 'There is nothing to describe what it means if the prosecution case is true. Equally, perhaps even more so, there is nothing to describe what it means if they are not true and the defendant has been falsely accused. Either is an equally horrific idea. Please try to imagine what it would mean to anybody, and what it would do to anybody, to be falsely accused of such a catalogue as this. It is ineffable. There are no words for it. It is a nightmare from whichever side you view the case. We ask for justice for this young woman. No more – and certainly no less.'

Mr Hunt told the jury that they had heard a great deal of detailed medical evidence from experts, none of whom knew what had actually happened. 'They are best-guessing, and we do not have trials by experts best-guessing. We have trial by jury, and you have to decide what, if anything, happened that was criminal. When I ask for justice for this young woman, I ask you to ask yourselves in each case whether they have proved it.'

Mr Hunt said that the prosecution had repeatedly alleged that 'something was done to *that* child, or something caused *that* child to collapse, or something caused *that* child to die. Again and again when a medical explanation has been put forward, it has been pooh-poohed. We simply do not know what happened – no more, for all their attempts, do the experts. We are into the area of speculation, and speculation is the very stuff of which wrongful convictions are made. It is nothing more than best-guessing, and a guess is no basis on which to convict anybody of murder or attempted murder.'

Mr Hunt stressed that it was odd that, for all the many events claimed to have taken place at Grantham Hospital, there was not a single witness who claimed to have seen Allitt do anything wrong. There was only one witness, from an old people's nursing home, who claimed to have seen Allitt holding a syringe. But Mr Hunt said that that witness's evidence had been so dubious that no fair-minded member of a jury 'would hang a dog' on what had been alleged.

He said that notorious cases tended to produce people keen to jump on the bandwagon with an apparently improving memory – something, he said, which did not happen in real life. 'An improving memory doesn't happen, but sometimes the bandwagon effect does.'

Referring to the evidence given by the Crown's medical experts, Mr Hunt said that they had only been able to tell the court the state of current medical knowledge. But over the years too many miscarriages of justice had resulted from an expert's view of the outcome of laboratory tests or what scientific evidence added up to: years later, something new had turned up to 'upset the applecart'.

Mr Hunt said that much of the prosecution case had been devoted to an inexplicable series of deaths and collapses. But, he maintained, the evidence in many of those cases was 'thin and consistent with innocence' – simply because they had occurred amid other similar incidents, they had been lumped together to create a presumption that Allitt had been responsible for all of them.

He ended by saying: 'Please detach yourselves from the emotions of this case. Please examine quite separately each and every count with the utmost care. The prosecution reconstruction is a best-guess in most cases. There are flaws in its evidence – more than one impossible thing to believe, we would suggest. There would not be words to describe it if you convicted her and got it wrong. It would be indeed ineffable.'

But in his closing speech, John Goldring said that the spate of attacks on patients in Ward 4 was not the action of a normal person – no one could have a rational motive for such behaviour, nor should the jury try to seek one. There was potent evidence that Allitt was responsible for all those attacks, either by injecting drugs or by blocking the airways of children, possibly with a hand over the mouth and nose. The attacks were 'insidious and chilling,' Mr Goldring said. There had been a definite *pattern*.

With the end of the closing speeches for both sides, the trial judge, Mr Justice Latham, began his necessarily lengthy and laborious summing-up. It took him two days to cover all the evidence.

Finally, on 11 May, the jury were sent out, Mr Justice Latham telling them that he was anxious that they should return unanimous verdicts on all the charges. That too would be a lengthy process. After four and a half hours of deliberation without a single verdict, the jury were sent to a hotel for the night, ready to resume their deliberations the following morning. What made it all the more difficult for them was that Allitt had not given evidence in her own defence. One gathers that the jury bent over backwards not to be unfair to her, a defendant who had been absent for most of the trial, prevented from giving testimony which might have swayed them one way or the other.

In the afternoon of 13 May, after almost sixteen hours of deliberation and at the end of a twelve-week trial, the jury returned with guilty verdicts in the murders of Becky Phillips and Claire Peck. The jury also found Allitt guilty of causing grievous bodily harm with intent to Kayley Desmond, Henry Chan and Christopher King. But they acquitted her of attempting to murder those three children. The guilty verdicts were greeted with gasps of relief and some cheering from the public gallery, while relatives of the children concerned wept quietly.

Allitt was informed of the verdicts by her solicitor, who phoned her at Rampton top-security hospital.

Meanwhile, the weary jury of seven men and five women were sent to a hotel for a third night to resume deliberations on the eighteen outstanding charges.

On Friday, 14 May, they returned to court briefly to deliver another verdict. They had found Allitt guilty of the murder of a third child, Liam Taylor. Later that day, they found her guilty of attempting to murder Brad Gibson and of causing grievous bodily harm, with intent, to Patrick Elstone.

On Saturday, they delivered yet more verdicts. They found Allitt guilty of attempting to murder Paul Crampton, but cleared her of attempting to murder Dorothy Lowe and Jonathan Jobson, also acquitting her of causing them grievous bodily harm with intent.

It was on Monday, 17 May, after six days of deliberation, that the jury came back with the final verdicts. They convicted Allitt of murdering Tim Hardwick, attempting to murder Katie Phillips, and causing grievous bodily harm, with intent, to Christopher Peasgood and Michael Davidson.

In thanking the jurors for their efforts, the judge offered them stress-counselling after their long ordeal. He told them: 'Very few – if any – juries have had to deal with so many matters which have caused such distress.'

At the end of the trial, after the prosecution revealed that Allitt was suffering from the Munchausen-by-proxy syndrome, Mr Justice Latham called on the Department of Health and Trent Regional Health Authority to explain why nothing was apparently done after a physiotherapist at the hospital reported her suspicions of that fact. The Health Secretary, Virginia Bottomley, announced an immediate inquiry, saying: 'It is vital that the lessons of this dreadful case are learnt and acted upon without delay,' and the health authority offered immediate ex-gratia compensation payments of over £1 million to the parents of the victims.

The row rumbles on. The Government refuses to hold

a *public* inquiry, as the parents demand. The two Ward 4 consultants involved in the case, Nelson Porter and Charith Nanayakkara, were made redundant in April 1993, following a reorganization at the hospital. They feel they have been made scapegoats for the crimes of Beverley Allitt, and plan to sue Grantham Hospital for reinstatement.

On 28 May, Allitt was brought to Nottingham Crown Court for the first time in two months, flanked by seven prison warders. It was eleven days since she had been convicted of her long catalogue of crimes. Looking thin and gaunt, she sat in the dock with her eyes downcast, showing not a flicker of emotion as Mr Justice Latham, who had listened to medical evidence about her, imposed thirteen life-sentences: four for the murders, three for the attempted murders, and a further six for the convictions of causing grievous bodily harm to other children. He told her: 'You have been convicted of the most terrible crimes. You are cunning and manipulative and you have shown no remorse for the trail of destruction you have left behind you – although I accept that that is a consequence of your severe personality disorder. You are and will be a very great danger to others, and there is very little chance of your ever being released.'

As Allitt was taken from the dock, there were cries of 'You bastard!' and 'Cage her!' from the public gallery. Allitt will indeed be caged, but it is now up to the Home Secretary to decide whether she serves her life sentences in prison or hospital.

But *can* a hospital cope with her? There are reports that she is enjoying lesbian relationships inside Rampton. Certainly she has written letters to her parents and friends, talking in enthusiastic terms about a new friend and saying: 'She has a nice bod.' Allitt is a very manipulative person, and has even tried to win officers round to her side. For that reason, shift rotas have been altered to ensure that no officer is exposed to her for too long.

On ancient maps, the unknown regions used to be left blank, with a warning message: 'Here be monsters.'

Beverley Allitt is a contemporary monster, a nightmare gargoyle of our time. Only one thing about her is certain: it will never be safe to release her upon the community.

The Habit of Murder

IT'S A MATTER OF TASTE. I have not changed my mind on the subject of mass-murderers since 1987 or so, when I remarked that, 'as a rule, mass-murderers [who used sometimes to be called "multicides"; the term "serial killers" is now so much the rage that it must soon be out of date] are dull: the minute that murdering becomes a habit, the murderer, usually a nonentity to start with, usually becomes a caricature of a human being; a murder should be as special an event to the murderer as it is to the victim. I can think of only a few exceptions to the rule: William Palmer (who gave lethal meaning to the betting term "winning accumulator"); George Joseph Smith (he would deserve immortality even if he had not made his brides momentarily more blushing by entering the bathrooms while they were bathing), Burke & Hare, and perhaps a couple more.'

However, likes and dislikes are often associated with, even transmutations of, other likes or dislikes; and they may have been caused, partly or wholly, by mental deficiencies. For all I know, I would find mass-murderers less dull, perhaps not at all dull, if, for instance, my mind did not panic, and therefore go blank, when required suddenly to memorize a catalogue of names (of victims), dates and places.

Anyway, as my ho-hum attitude to mass-murders in general means that my knowledge of this subject within a subject is paltry, I asked two crime-historian friends, both experts on the sub-subject, to contribute something about it. At that time, one of them, Richard Whittington-Egan, had, with his wife Molly, recently completed a book called *The Murder Almanac* (published later in 1992 by Neil Wilson, Glasgow), and he suggested that I should quote from the book's introduction the following sub-division of the sub-subject.

What exactly *is* a serial killer? How does he differ from a mass-murderer? Is it simply a matter of semantics? Both, surely, are multiple murderers? They are. The determining diagnostic feature has to be the psychological motivation of the killer. The mass-murderer kills numbers of people for any one, or any combination, of the classic motives: gain, revenge, elimination, jealousy, conviction, which is to say killing for an idea or an ideal. The serial killer kills primarily for a compulsive sexual reason, or for pure love and lust for killing; although, of course, just to make things more complicated, incidental benefits may accrue to be taken advantage of.

The other friend, Wilfred Gregg, made the following list of The Ten Most Prolific Serial Killers (treating a partnership as one) – but stressed that it was based on source materials which, in many cases, either exaggerated or understated (and it was usually impossible to say which) the true tally.

PEDRO LOPEZ (Arrested in 1980.)	Colombia, Ecuador, Peru	300+
GILLES DE RAIS – 'BLUEBEARD' (Executed in 1440.)	France	140+
HENRY LEE LUCAS (Soon after his arrest in 1983, he confessed to more than 360 murders; but he then withdrew the confessions. He has so far been convicted of 11 murders. The total here ascribed to him is the 'guesstimate' of police authorities.)	USA	100+

BRUNO LUDKE	Germany	85
(Executed in 1944.)		
DELFINA AND MARIA GONZALES	Mexico	80+
(Arrested in 1964.)		
DANIEL BARBOSA	Colombia,	71
(Arrested in 1988.)	Ecuador	
JANE TOPPAN	USA	31–70
(Arrested in 1901, and kept in an asylum until her death in 1938.)		
DONALD HARVEY	USA	57
(Arrested in 1987.)		
MARIE DE BRINVILLIERS	France	50+
(Executed in 1676.)		
'THE GREEN RIVER KILLER'	USA	49
(Never arrested for murders committed near Green River, Seattle, 1982–4.)		

Since that list was made, a French 'court of honour' has concluded that Gilles de Rais (who in his younger days fought the English alongside Joan of Arc) was innocent of murder; but as the conclusion seems to be largely based upon the never-doubted fact that 'Bluebeard' was tortured into confessing, which doesn't mean that the entire confession was false, it would not be sensible to delete his name from the list unless and until the conclusion has been verified by honourable experts. However, a new name has had to be entered, causing the relegation of the Green River Killer.

Andrei Chikatilo is – perhaps, by the time this book appears, *was* – a Russian, living in Rostov-on-Don, two hundred miles north of the Black Sea. Born in that city in 1935, he gained a degree in literature, became a school-teacher, married a local woman, who bore him two children, and wrote articles for local papers on the rearing of children as good communists. Some time after 1978 (in which year a hideously brutal, sexually-motivated murder of a young woman was committed in one of the forests that skirt Rostov; a man named Alexander Kravchenko was found guilty of the crime and executed), Chikatilo gave up teaching and took a job with a manufacturing concern which required him occasionally to travel to faraway places such as Moscow and Leningrad.

Other murders, bearing strong similarities to the one that had been officially solved, were committed in the woods around Rostov; also in faraway places such as Moscow and Leningrad. The police realized that a serial killer was at work or play; but either the police or certain politicians to whom they answered decided against making the realization public. Perhaps the decision was taken so as not to cause alarm; or perhaps the knowledge was kept secret for fear of blemishing the image of the communist state. There were further murders, clearly continuing the serial, which eventually spanned the dozen years from 1978.

During that time, a number of men, most of them residents of Rostov, came under suspicion, were interrogated, and were released. Andrei Chikatilo was among them. He was interrogated on two occasions. The main, perhaps sole, reason why he was suspected seems to have been that he was in Moscow and in Leningrad when murders of the serial kind were committed in those cities; no evidence was found on or in any of the corpses or at the scene of any of the murders which was considered by policemen or forensic scientists to be of possible use in linking the crimes to the criminal.

Towards the end of 1990 – shortly before the Soviet Union was disbanded – he was arrested again. After an interrogative period – of hours, according to one report, of days on end, according to another – Chikatilo, who was bespectacled, of medium height and build, neatly dressed, and with hair, once mouse-coloured but now mostly grey, combed primly from a parting on the right-hand side, confessed that he had committed 52 murders, the first of them the crime for which Alexander Kravchenko had been executed. 21 of the victims were male, none past his teens, the youngest only eight. None of the 31 female victims was over thirty, and 14 were adolescent.

Chikatilo said that all his victims had accompanied him of their own accord to wherever he had murdered them; speaking of a 'double event', the murder of a mother and her daughter, he said that he had lured them to a forest-glade by lying that he owned a *dacha* (country cottage) and offering hospitality there. It appears that, if he was asked (surely he was) why he had taken up killing, what had caused him to continue, he could not or would not explain. He mentioned that he had always been greatly affected by something he had heard as a child – that, during the Ukrainian famine of that time, a cousin of his, a peasant in the region, had either died from starvation or been slaughtered by other peasants, who had then eaten him. One gathers that Chikatilo had been sexually impotent since some time after his wife's pregnancy with their second child. It is unclear whether that information came from him or from his wife, who said that he was a loving husband and father, and at first refused to believe that he could have inflicted the slightest physical harm on anybody, on any living thing, even a fly. She has since moved from Rostov to some undisclosed location, where she lives incognito. Presumably the children, themselves parents, have taken similar precautions.

Prior to the trial, which did not start till the spring of 1992, doctors from the Serbsky Institute, Moscow, the best-known seat of psychiatric learning in Russia, decided unanimously that, according to the legal defini-tion of sanity, Chikatilo was as sane as they were; respon-sible for his homicidal actions, and therefore answerable for them. Specially for the trial, in a court-house in Rostov, a cage of steel bars was built to accommodate the defendant. As the bars were about a foot apart, with no missile-proof material between them, the cage must have been intended as protection from Chikatilo rather than as protection for him from any vengeful relatives of the victims who might try to take the law into their own hands. Although, each day, relatives outnumbered the (also-crammed) other spectators in the public part of the court, and although some of them occasionally hurled abuse and made threatening gestures at Chikatilo, there seem to be no reports of efforts to harm him while the evidence was being given.

Either he had gone completely bald during the long time since his arrest or, at his wish or in accordance with a prison regulation, his head had been shaved. Ensuring that he could not injure himself other than by banging his head on the steel bars (which he did more than once, though never forcefully enough to produce a bruise), he was permitted to wear only a few garments, all casual, without tie, belt or shoe-laces, and had to leave his spectacles outside the cage. The fact that he was not even allowed underpants was revealed when, without apparent appropriateness to the concurrent testimony, he stripped naked and toyed with his private parts. He often behaved eccentrically in other ways – for instance, by walking on tip-toe around and around the perimeter of the cage while staring intently at a point in the centre of its floor . . . by screaming mixtures of incoherence and oaths at no one or nothing in particular . . . by bellowing laughter that stopped as suddenly as it had started, his face expressionless meanwhile.

There was nothing to laugh at in the testimony. The witnesses, more than two hundred of them, mostly policemen and doctors, spoke of atrocities: bodies of young people, hands and legs bound, that had been smashed with hammers, stabbed and lacerated with large knives; the killer had bitten off tips of tongues and parts of sexual organs – and had (so it was implied from the negative searches of the surrounding areas) eaten them.

The trial went on for six months, till the middle of October 1992, the day before Chikatilo's fifty-seventh birthday. In his summing-up, the judge said: 'It is clear that negligence by the law enforcement agencies played a major role in allowing Chikatilo to remain at large for so long' – an assertion that must have made the leaders of the investigation worry that they themselves might become the subject of an investigation, since such negligence is a criminal offence, carrying severe penalties, in Russia. Having made the verdict clear from the start of his speech, the judge passed sentence of death, omitting the words 'by shooting', which was taken to mean that he considered the usual method of execution, the firing of a bullet through the back of the head, too humane for Chikatilo.

The announcement of the sentence provoked screams of jubilation from among the spectators, some of whom tried, without succeeding, to breach the cordon of policemen around the cage. Perhaps because Chikatilo was shocked by the sudden tumult, the flashing of press cameras, and the directing of television lights at the cage, his eyes widened and his lips moved; on the other hand, perhaps reporters were such expert lip-readers that they were correct in saying that 'he screamed defiance and hate'. As soon as the court was cleared, he was removed from the cage and taken back to the high-security prison where he had till now shared a cell with a man on remand for currency speculation.

Immediately after the trial, Chikatilo's lawyer announced that there would be an appeal on two grounds: that, never mind what the psychiatrists had decided, Chikatilo was insane, and that the prosecution had failed to produce sufficient evidence in corroboration of his (admittedly extremely detailed) confession. Other lawyers commented that, though the appeal was likely to fail, Chikatilo might not be executed. Coincidentally, at about the time his trial began, a presidential commission, made up of writers and human-rights activists, had begun discussing whether or not capital punishment should be abolished; since then, it had commuted all but one of the 46 death sentences that were pending.

The 'Fatal Attraction' Murder

ALBERT BOROWITZ

Even before the facts were known in detail, journalists as well as the police had decided that the case of Carolyn Warmus showed that Nature was up to her old trick of imitating Art. Within days of Warmus's indictment in February 1990 for the murder of her lover's wife, Betty Jeanne Solomon, a year before, the press labelled the prosecution a real-life 'Fatal Attraction' case, identifying the defendant with the character played frighteningly by Glenn Close in the popular 1987 movie that happened to have been filmed in Westchester County, to the north of New York City, where Mrs Solomon was killed. In the view of *New York Times* film critic Caryn James, it was 'safe to guess that Glenn Close made Carolyn Warmus the celebrity she is today.'

The parallel that reporters drew between the murder of Betty Jeanne Solomon and the 'Fatal Attraction' film was hard to resist, because the police and the prosecution shaped the image of blonde Carolyn Warmus as a woman obsessed with her former lover, Paul Solomon, who had wanted the freedom to move on to other infidelities. The police investigators released stories that Warmus had, since her college years, established a pattern of pursuing married or unavailable men.

The daughter of a wealthy insurance executive, Warmus grew up in suburban Detroit and received her undergraduate degree in psychology from the University of Michigan. Her classmates recalled that she took her dates with Paul Laven, a pre-med teaching assistant, so seriously that she became a convert to his religion, Judaism. When, however, Laven broke off the relationship and became engaged to another woman, Warmus undertook a relentless campaign to win him back. She called the couple and left long messages on their answering machine, annoyed their friends, and deluged them with notes. One message, left on the windshield of Laven's car, falsely claimed that Carolyn was pregnant and begged him to call her. Another, sent to Laven's fiancée and filled with misspellings to disguise Warmus's authorship, insisted that the woman stood no chance of competing with Carolyn's more voluptuous figure and newly-acquired tan. Finally, the couple were forced to obtain a restraining order against their persecutor in a Michigan court to ensure that she would not attempt to ruin their wedding.

After her college graduation, Carolyn Warmus moved to New York City, where she earned a master's degree in education from Teacher's College at Columbia University and went on to serve as a substitute in school districts of Westchester County for teachers who were on maternity leaves. In the New York area the skein of romantic fixations which had begun back home in Michigan continued to lengthen. She hired a private detective, Vincent Parco, to trail a married New Jersey bartender whose affection for her had slackened. Together, she and Parco devised the idea of superimposing photographs of Warmus in sexy poses on to pictures of the bartender, apparently with the intention of mailing the resulting montages to his wife. Parco was just the man for such a deception, since he taught a Learning Annex course to aspiring snoops, entitled 'How to Get Anything on Anybody'. Inculcating the priceless lessons of his craft in classes held on the premises of Manhattan's swanky Birch Wathen School, Parco taught his students how to hide a video camera in a purse or a looseleaf notebook, and how to obtain unlisted telephone numbers by consulting reverse directories or examining registration records at the Board of Elections.

The collaboration of Warmus with Parco was a blending of kindred spirits, because the young teacher was herself adept in fraud and forgery. She successfully carried off her first swindle after her graduation from college, when she was working as a waitress at the Jukebox, a popular 1950s-style dance club in Royal Oak, Michigan. The club manager, Debbie Mullins, explained to a *Newsday* reporter how Warmus's scheme was accomplished:

> Warmus was accused of running credit cards through an imprinting machine two or three times, using one imprint for the credit card customer and the others for customers who would pay in cash. Warmus . . . would then pocket the cash she collected rather than put it into the till. Mullins charges that Warmus stole thousands of dollars. Federal agents were brought in to investigate, but they could not find enough evidence to bring charges against her.

Several years later, Carolyn again had recourse to forgery, this time to establish an alibi as a defence to a damage claim. In 1987, a woman identifying herself as Carolyn Warmus was involved in an automobile accident. Subsequently, Warmus wrote to the other driver involved, stating that she had been chaperoning a school trip in Washington on the day of the accident and offering as proof a letter signed by a school official, Dr Richard Sprague. Later Sprague denied both that he had written the letter and that Warmus had attended the class trip to which she had referred.

In September 1987 Carolyn Warmus, then twenty-three, met Paul Solomon, who was thirty-eight, when she began teaching at the Greenville School in the Edgemont School District in Greenburgh, Westchester County; she later moved on to the Byram Hills School District in nearby Armonk, where she taught computer science, but Solomon remained at the Greenville School. Betty Jeanne Solomon, Paul's wife, was an account executive with the Continental Credit Corporation in Harrison,

New York, and she and her husband lived with their daughter Kristan (thirteen years old in 1987) in a condominium on South Central Avenue in Greenburgh. The marriage bond between the Solomons was apparently not very strong: Paul admits to having had two brief affairs before meeting Carolyn Warmus, and he suspected Betty Jeanne of carrying on a relationship of several years with her former boss.

Some months after their first meeting, Carolyn Warmus and Paul Solomon embarked on an affair which featured sexual encounters in her apartment above the comedy club 'Catch a Rising Star' on Manhattan's east side, as well as in hotel rooms and Warmus's car. Doing her best to keep the liaison a secret, Warmus took on the role of a friend of the whole Solomon family, showering Kristan with gifts and taking her on a skiing trip. It was on this excursion that Warmus confessed to the teenager a fear that Betty Jeanne Solomon did not like her very much. Kristan tried to persuade her to the contrary, but 'deep down' she knew that Warmus's concern was well-founded. In August 1988, when Paul Solomon had briefly stopped seeing her, Warmus confided to a college friend, Ryan Attenson, of Southfield, Michigan, that her relationship was not 'progressing in a manner with which she was comfortable'; she spoke of her desire to engage a private investigator to prove to her errant lover that his wife was cheating on him.

Shortly before midnight on Sunday evening, 15 January 1989, police in Greenburgh received a call from Paul Solomon, who had returned home to find his wife murdered. Betty Jeanne was lying on the living-room floor; she had been pistol-whipped about the head and had nine bullet wounds in her back and legs. None of the neighbours had heard the shots, there was no sign of forced entry, and the only indication of a struggle was a disconnected telephone; police photographed a black woollen glove near the corpse.

At first, the investigation focused on Paul Solomon. After initially telling Greenburgh detectives that he had spent the evening bowling near his home, he admitted that he had stopped only briefly at the bowling alley and had spent the evening with Carolyn Warmus at the Holiday Inn in Yonkers, New York. After drinks in the motel's Treetops Lounge, followed by hamburgers, french fries and some oysters, the couple had repaired to Warmus's red Hyundai car, in which, as she later told the police, they performed a sex act; Carolyn specified in her statement that during their lovemaking she occupied the driver's seat. Witnesses came forward to confirm that they had seen Solomon at the bowling alley and later in Warmus's company at the Holiday Inn.

After some months, police suspicions shifted from Solomon to Warmus. One of the reasons for heightened interest in Carolyn was evidence of her relentless pursuit of Paul Solomon after the murder. In June 1989, after Solomon broke off his relations with Warmus, she followed him to Puerto Rico, where he was vacationing with a new girlfriend, Barbara Ballor. Posing as a police officer, she called Ballor's family from the island, urging them to end the romance. An even more startling development in the investigation was receipt of a tip that in early January 1989, shortly before the murder, Carolyn had purchased from private-eye Vincent Parco a handgun equipped with a silencer.

On 2 February 1989 Carolyn Warmus was indicted for second-degree murder and the possession of an unregistered firearm. Six months later, however, the indictment was dismissed by Judge John Carey, on the ground that the state had not disclosed to the grand jury the fact that Vincent Parco had been granted immunity from prosecution in exchange for his agreement to testify about his sale of the pistol to Warmus. The prosecutors promptly obtained a fresh indictment, and the widely heralded 'Fatal Attraction' trial of Carolyn Warmus opened on Thursday, 14 February 1991, in Westchester County Courthouse, where headmistress Jean S. Harris of Madeira School had been convicted of murdering

Dr Herman Tarnower a decade earlier. The prosecution team was headed by thirty-eight-year-old Assistant District Attorney James A. McCarty, and David L. Lewis defended Carolyn Warmus. Lewis was president of the New York Association of Criminal Defence Lawyers and a director of the National Association of Criminal Lawyers; he had acted as a trial lawyer for the former Panamanian dictator, General Manuel Noriega, and was accustomed to trying cases in the limelight. Judge John Carey presided, and a jury of eight women and four men was selected. The jurors scanned with understandable interest the features of the celebrated defendant, whose appearance was described by the *Newsday* reporter with a mixture of attentive observation and prurient imaginings:

> Her thick blonde hair is cut in a neat, chin-length chop. Just enough makeup coats her milky-white skin to hide a large crop of freckles. It is easy to imagine her long legs, hidden by a modest black skirt, in the gym shorts and sneakers of her athletic, teenage years.
>
> But then the smile is oddly cut short by a hard blink of her eyes and a quick, convulsive grimace. It is a startling, spasmodic reaction, almost a nervous tic – and it periodically breaks on the smooth planes of Carolyn Warmus's face. Her apparent confidence is gone for an instant, and in its place one sees a flash of the troubled history that has been so widely reported in the media since she was indicted a year ago.

In his opening statement, prosecutor McCarty told the jury that Warmus was driven by a 'consuming desire to possess' Paul Solomon. The evidence was circumstantial but, 'like pieces of a puzzle . . . would reveal a clear picture of the killer of Betty Jeanne Solomon: the defendant, Carolyn Warmus'. The proof would include testimony from private investigator Parco, who had sold Warmus a gun and silencer, as well as telephone company records of a call on the day of the slaying made from the defendant's apartment to a gunshop where she later bought bullets, using as false identification a driver's licence that she had stolen from a secretary in an office where Warmus worked in the summer of 1988. The Solomons' marriage had had its ups and downs over the years, McCarty admitted; both husband and wife were having affairs, but they were 'not ready to call it quits'. In the summer of 1988, after Solomon temporarily ended his relationship with Carolyn Warmus, she wrote him notes, gave his daughter Kristan extravagant gifts, and told her college friend Ryan Attenson that Paul Solomon was the perfect person for her. The only obstacle was Betty Jeanne Solomon, and the defendant had made it clear to Attenson that she would do anything to get her out of the picture so that she could take her place in the household.

David L. Lewis responded for the defence by arguing that the case was not about the impropriety of Warmus's adulterous affair, and that her love for Paul Solomon did not demonstrate her guilt. There was no physical evidence, he emphasized, to show that Warmus was in the Solomons' home on the night of the killing. Charging that the prosecution was hampered by sloppy police work, Lewis strongly suggested that Paul Solomon and private detective Vincent Parco were responsible for the murder and for faking evidence to incriminate Carolyn Warmus. When the defence counsel took his seat at the end of his address, the jury was left to wonder how he would support his conspiracy allegations.

Early in the prosecution's case, two Greenburgh police officers related their impressions of Paul Solomon's mental state when they questioned him at the murder scene. Patrol officer Michael Cotter described Paul as shaken: 'He said he rolled her over and saw all the blood and started crying; he cried again when he looked at the blood on his hands.' In cross-examining the two officers, David Lewis attacked the police for losing possible traces of evidence that might have pointed to other suspects. One of the trial reporters agreed, comparing the Greenburgh police to the Keystone Kops; Paul Solomon had been allowed to wash his hands, and the black glove that was pictured in a police photograph had subsequently vanished and could not be located at the time of the trial.

Lewis had limited success in his efforts to weaken the testimony of Carolyn Warmus's friend Ryan Attenson, to whom she had spoken of the setback in her relationship with Paul Solomon in August 1988. In a telephone conversation, she had asserted that 'with her money and Paul's family' (by which Attenson assumed she was referring to the Solomons' teenage daughter Kristan) 'they would have a perfect life together.' She said that she 'would take it upon herself to make sure that she ended up' with her lover. Several months after the killing but before her arrest, Warmus had spoken to Attenson again; on this occasion she informed him that Solomon and she were going to end up together and that everything had been taken care of – the other woman was no longer an obstacle. Under cross-examination, Attenson conceded that he did not remember Warmus's exact words but was relating the essence of what she had told him.

Kristan Solomon held the courtroom spellbound with her account of Warmus's campaign to win her goodwill. Paul Solomon had introduced Kristan, an athlete who competed in several sports, to Warmus when he was coaching his daughter and her teammates during an after-school basketball practice. During the next few months she had chatted with Warmus in her classroom, seen her at basketball games, and gone to a Christmas show in Manhattan with her father, Warmus and another teacher. It was in early 1988, when she and her parents had gone out to dinner with Carolyn Warmus, that the defendant had offered to take her skiing during the winter break. Kristan also told the jury about the birthday gifts that she had received from the defendant. On the girl's fifteenth birthday in August 1988, when the prosecutors asserted that Solomon had temporarily broken off their affair, Warmus had unexpectedly arrived at the

Solomons' condominium with two outfits and a bracelet for Kristan. 'I was in shock,' Kristan testified. 'I was not frightened but hesitant, because I knew my Mom didn't enjoy her in the house, and I was worried there would be words.' After Betty Jeanne's death, Warmus had left notes on the door of the Solomons' condominium but had not seen Kristan; however, two weeks before the girl's sixteenth birthday, she had arrived home to discover a pale blue Tiffany's box at her doorstep containing diamond stud-earrings and a note from Warmus signed, 'Love always, Carolyn.'

Prosecution lawyers began their efforts to tie Warmus to the murder weapon with the testimony of a private investigator, James A. Russo, who swore that the defendant had consulted him a few months before the slaying to seek protection from a woman named 'Jean or Betty Jean,' who was trying to hurt her family. When Russo had suggested a bodyguard, Warmus had stated her preference for a 'machine gun and silencer'. On three earlier occasions in the late summer and early fall of 1988, Warmus had consulted Russo about other fears. During one of her interviews she had claimed that her father's jet had been sabotaged in Michigan and that a 'woman was seen in the vicinity in the hangar'; during her next visit, Warmus had told Russo that the same woman had struck her sister's car in Washington in a hit-and-run. In his cross-examination, Lewis tried to discredit Russo by portraying him as a sleazy detective who would do anything for money. At his prodding, the witness recounted his recent work for a landlord who suspected a prostitution ring in his upper eastside apartment building; the witness said he had 'gone undercover' and paid a prostitute $400 in exchange for sex.

Dramatic evidence of the murder night was provided by an operator of the New York Telephone Company. Since a direct police emergency network was not established in Westchester County, customers who dialled 911 were answered by a private operator who then referred messages to the local police. Shortly before 7.12 on the night of the killing, the witness, Linda Viana Newcombe, had received a call from a screaming woman whose only decipherable words sounded like 'trying to kill me'. The call was quickly disconnected and the operator, now thoroughly rattled, had transposed the digits of the number of the telephone on which the incoming call had been made; because of this mistake she had reported the emergency to the Scarsdale police, who had then rerouted the message to the Greenburgh station. David Lewis attempted without success to have the witness specify whether the caller had said '*he* is trying to kill me' or '*she* is trying to kill me'.

On 8 February, Paul Solomon, who had been granted immunity from prosecution, took the stand to tell the jury about his strained marriage of nineteen years, his feelings of guilt over the affair with Carolyn Warmus, and his actions on the murder night, culminating in the discovery of his wife's body. He had not had sex with Carolyn Warmus in the summer of 1988, but in the fall they had resumed relations despite his conflicting feelings. When they had met for drinks at the Holiday Inn in Yonkers, Paul told the jury, he had encouraged Warmus to seek her happiness elsewhere:

> She said it was difficult finding good people to date. I said, 'I'd be so happy to dance at your wedding and see you happy.' She said, 'What about *your* happiness, Paul? Don't *you* deserve to be happy?' And I said, 'If anything happens to Betty Jeanne and me, I'd never get married anyway.'

Despite this exercise in dissuasion, he had then accompanied her to her car to have sexual relations.

For months after his wife's death, Solomon had not seen Warmus and had begun dating a new girlfriend. After playing basketball in Manhattan in July 1989, he had stopped by Warmus's eastside apartment. At a nearby bar he had asked her whether she had had anything to do with Betty Jeanne's death. She had replied that she was pleased he felt 'comfortable enough' to ask her that, but said she had had no involvement. Solomon had asked her again later and she had repeated her denial; he told the jury that he had 'absolutely believed her'. Prosecutor McCarty elicited Solomon's story of how Warmus had followed him and his new girlfriend to Puerto Rico eight months after the murder, even though he had never told her of his vacation plans. He had become so 'frightened' when she appeared on the scene that he had notified hotel security, called the Greenburgh police, and left that night.

At the start of his cross-examination, Warmus's lawyer David Lewis held up a card that Solomon had given the defendant early in their affair. Its passionate terms contrasted with Warmus's banal messages about school and community events. The note read:

> If you're smart you'll do one of two things. Turn away
> and never see me again and save yourself from the
> pain and hurt, or keep loving me and take the risk
> of you and I having something together forever.

A lot of people write cards, Solomon stated defensively under Lewis's questioning, and sometimes 'people put down things that others put more into.' The witness's constant reliance on qualifications cannot have strengthened his testimony in the jury's minds. Asked at one point whether he spoke Russian, Solomon replied, 'Not that I'm aware of.'

On the fifth and final day of his cross-examination on 21 February, Solomon burst into a rage when David Lewis bluntly suggested that he was involved in the killing. Calling the insinuation 'obscene,' the witness charged the defence counsel with an inclination to 'twist and turn words, manipulate facts or half-truths and incomplete reports, to make them what they aren't.'

Following Solomon to the stand was investigator Vincent Parco, who had also been granted immunity in exchange for his testimony. Parco stated that Warmus had badgered him for months to provide her with a gun to protect her against burglars who were ravaging her eastside neighbourhood. Succumbing at last to her insistence, in the first week of January 1989 he had sold her an unregistered black Beretta .25 calibre pistol, a homemade silencer and a dozen bullets for $2,500 in cash delivered in three separate envelopes. It was Parco's suggestion that he have the silencer made – so that she could 'practice in the woods, the house, in relative obscurity.' The detective was able to locate a Brooklyn machine-tool operator, George Peters, who had agreed to mill the silencer in accordance with diagrams in a book, *How to Make a Silencer*, which Parco had obtained from his friend Rocco Lovetere. Parco, ever the perfectionist, was dissatisfied with the performance of Peters's silencer (which he had tested by firing into a tree in lower Manhattan) and had insisted on alterations.

The day after the murder, Carolyn had called to tell Parco that some teacher had been 'stabbed or bludgeoned eight or nine times'; the police had come to question her, and she had hidden the gun inside one of the posts of her brass bed. Parco had offered to pick up the gun the next day, but Warmus had told him that the weapon was gone; she had thrown it off a parkway.

Judge John Carey had excluded as prejudicial any testimony relating to Warmus's engagement of Parco to aid her persecution of the New Jersey bartender, or any other evidence indicating that she had obsessively pursued men prior to her affair with Solomon. However, Parco admitted that he had become infatuated with his attractive client – although he stoutly insisted that he had rejected her sexual advances. Parco also stated that in August 1989 Carolyn Warmus had asked him to check out a licence plate and a telephone number. The phone number belonged to a woman Solomon had started dating, while the licence was for her father's car. During the summer of 1989 Warmus had denied any relationship with Paul Solomon and had told Parco she was out bowling with a 'bunch of teachers' on the night of the murder.

Defence attorney Lewis subjected Parco to a day-long cross-examination, eliciting admissions that as a

110

private investigator he often used disguises and false names, and, in order to obtain information, engaged in deceptive practices known in the trade as 'gags'. In a surprising show of modesty, though, Parco refused to rate himself an expert in assuming an 'acting role' in his undercover work.

On 5 March a *Newsday* reporter, who regarded the prosecution's evidence to that point as flimsy, disclosed that Paul Solomon stood to gain $120,000, more than twice his annual salary, if a movie was made about the case. A week later the case took a turn in the prosecution's favour with the testimony of Patricia January, a nurse at the Bedford Road Elementary School in Pleasantville, New York, who swore that a week before the killing of Betty Jeanne Solomon, Warmus, after completing a telephone call from the school, had told her that she was 'terrified' to live alone and had a gun. According to the nurse, Warmus had added that 'of course' she would never kill anyone, and didn't have ammunition; she had also mentioned that the gun was 'specially made' by a private detective. Defence attorney Lewis told Judge Carey that he was surprised by the testimony and obtained an adjournment. In two hours of cross-examination when the court reconvened, Lewis focused on why Patricia January had waited so long to tell authorities of her conversation. The nurse had two answers: She had thought it was common knowledge that Carolyn owned the gun and, besides, she had 'wanted someone to open the door' for her to talk about the incident.

After Patricia January was excused from the stand, the opposing legal teams girded themselves for the principal evidentiary battle of the trial, a clash between inconsistent telephone records for 15 January 1989, the day of the murder. A microfiche, obtained by the prosecution from the MCI telephone service that Warmus used, showed a call from her apartment at 3.02 p.m. to Ray's Sport Shop, where bullets were purchased later that afternoon. In response, David Lewis, bringing to the fore at last his principal evidence of a conspiracy to incriminate his client, offered a document that he claimed to be the original MCI bill received by Warmus for January 1989. This document, printed in an MCI bill format and bearing the company's logo, lacked the call to Ray's Sport Shop on 15 January but included a direct-dial call at 6.44 p.m. on the same day that brought the total telephone charge to the same figure shown in the MCI record. Lewis told the judge that the 6.44 call 'made it all but impossible for [Warmus] to have been in Westchester at 7.15 to commit the murder.' The prosecution mounted a devastating attack on the authenticity of the 'bill' offered by the defence, showing that the MCI record it had introduced was consistent with the company's computer tapes and that the paper on which the defence version of the bill was prepared lacked a slogan that was imprinted on all MCI customer statements in January 1989. Ultimately Judge Carey permitted both versions of the disputed telephone bill to be submitted to the jury.

In the days that followed, the prosecution completed its chain of evidence. Liisa Kattai, a secretary for a telecommunications company, identified Warmus as a temporary office employee who had worked with her in August 1988, when Kattai had noticed that her New York State driver's licence was missing. According to Kattai, Warmus resembled the witness's photograph taken for her driver's licence at a time that she had shorter, 'frosted' blonde hair. It was the prosecution's theory that Warmus had posed as Kattai when she purchased ammunition at the gunshop on the afternoon before the murder. Subsequently, Detective Joseph Reich of the Westchester County Police testified that he had compared six shell casings found at the murder scene with a seventh picked up eleven months later in the Brooklyn machine shop of George Peters, who had admitted milling a silencer at Parco's request; all seven bullets had been fired from the same gun.

The testimony for the defence began with trucker Anthony Gambino, who supported Lewis's conspiracy theory by stating that Parco had asked him to commit a murder in the summer of 1988; he had virtuously declined the request. Another witness implicating Parco in the crime was Joseph Lisella, who stated that, from a stall in the men's room of a bowling alley where he had stopped between 7.30 and 8.30 p.m. on 15 January 1989, he had heard two men exchange $20,000 and talk about having thrown a gun in the 'deepest part of the river'. He had not seen the men's faces, but they had called each other Vinnie and Paul, the first names of Parco and Solomon. The conspiracy theme was pursued with the testimony of Thomas A. Warmus, the defendant's father, who stated that Parco had tried to shake him down for a substantial sum of money in the summer of 1989; Mr Warmus left the courtroom without having looked at his daughter. On 10 April, the defence rested after Lewis had shown the jury a news videotape of Parco making threatening remarks about Gambino after the trucker's testimony.

In the closing arguments, the prosecution claimed that it had established a persuasive chain of circumstantial evidence, while Lewis, pounding home his conspiracy theory, invoked the Salem witchcraft trials as a parallel to the unjust persecution of his client.

The jurors deliberated for twelve days, a record in Westchester County, and ultimately deadlocked, with eight reportedly in favour of conviction and four holding out for acquittal; Judge Carey regretfully declared a mistrial. Interviews with the jury revealed that the minority of the jurors who favoured acquittal were disturbed by the circumstantial nature of the evidence and could not believe that a woman could have brutally pistol-whipped Betty Jeanne as the murderer had done. All of the jurors agreed that the defence telephone bill was a fake, but the minority faction thought that the forgery might have been an act of desperation on the part of someone being framed for murder. One juror could not credit the possibility that Carolyn Warmus, given her inexperience with guns, could have hit a moving target with all nine bullets, even at close range.

When the second trial began in January 1992 (after an unsuccessful attempt by the state to have Judge Carey replaced on the ground that he was biased in favour of Warmus), the prosecution trial team and strategy remained intact, but the defence had been thoroughly overhauled. Warmus had hired a new lawyer, William I. Aronwald, whose low-key style was in stark contrast with the theatrical and bellicose manner of the defendant's original counsel, David Lewis. It was Aronwald's intention to cast suspicion on Paul Solomon and Vincent Parco, as Lewis had done, but the 'frame-up' theme would be subordinated to a broader plan to create reasonable doubt on a number of issues. Aronwald's less melodramatic approach was mandated by the first jury's obvious rejection of the principal evidence that Lewis had offered to show that the case against Warmus was pure fabrication. Even jurors who had held out for acquittal were persuaded that the telephone invoice introduced by the defence at the first trial was a fake and that two key defence witnesses, trucker Anthony Gambino and men's room eavesdropper Joseph Lisella, were not worthy of belief. After the first trial ended, the state indicted Warmus for forgery of the telephone bill; subsequently Judge Carey ruled that the prosecution could not introduce the alleged forgery into evidence at the second murder trial as proof of Warmus's consciousness of guilt, since she might have been unaware of the fabrication of the document.

The prosecution case appeared to be following its expected course until 4 March, when Westchester Assistant District Attorney James McCarty made a stunning announcement. He told the court that the black glove that had been photographed at the murder scene and later vanished had now been rediscovered. In January the prosecution had asked Paul Solomon to search again for evidence for the new trial, and he had delivered the glove, which he said he had found in a box in his bedroom closet. Forensic tests had turned up barely visible finger-shaped human bloodstains on top of the glove.

Unprepared for this turn of events, defence counsel Aronwald accused prosecutor McCarty of 'trial by ambush', and Judge Carey initially ruled the glove inadmissible. He was, however, promptly induced to rethink his stand when McCarty told him that he had procured credit-card and store records revealing that on 9 November 1987 Carolyn Warmus had purchased a pair of gloves at Filene's Basement in Greenburgh matching the glove found in the Solomon residence. Faced with this offer of proof, Judge Carey ruled that the glove could be admitted if the prosecution was able to show that Warmus had bought gloves 'having similar intrinsic characteristics' of colour, material, size and style.

The Filene's sales slip did not specify the colour of the gloves purchased but permitted their identification as Shalimar Vanity Glove Inc.'s style 6781, a $10 one-size-fits-all wool glove manufactured by a Chinese state-owned cooperative. The Solomons' daughter, Kristan, testified that Warmus had worn black gloves, and a forensic expert, Dr Peter DeForest, testified that, after comparing the fibres found in the victim's hand during the original murder investigation with the fibres of the glove, he had found the two sets to be 'indistinguishable'.

Satisfied that sufficient evidence had been established to link the glove to the murder and to the defendant, Judge Carey ruled that it could be admitted, but excluded any reference to the tests revealing that spatters on the glove might be human blood. To the bafflement of observers, defence counsel Aronwald himself highlighted the evidence of the apparent bloodstains by contending that Solomon might have placed the stains on the glove recently in an attempt to incriminate Carolyn Warmus.

The prosecution rested its case on 5 May, and the defence, shuffling the order of its witnesses to meet the menace posed by the black glove, called to the stand William Bohus, president of Shalimar Vanity Glove Inc., the importer of the gloves identified in the Filene's sales slip as purchased by Warmus. Bohus testified that his company had sold some 36,000 pairs of the gloves since 1986, a quarter of which were black. Carolyn Warmus's stepmother, Nancy K. Dailey, also gave evidence intended to minimize the impact of the prosecution's newly rediscovered glove. She showed the jurors a black and gold ski-suit, with its own matching black gloves, that she had bought for Carolyn long before the murder. Mrs Dailey's testimony seemed to prove only that Carolyn Warmus might have owned more than one pair of black gloves, and the prosecution was quick to emphasize this fashion note. The ski-suit was almost all black, prosecutor McCarty's assistant Douglas FitzMorris observed. Was black one of Ms Warmus's favourite colours? . . . Might she not have liked the colour so much that she had bought a second pair? . . . Wasn't she wearing black right now in the courtroom? According to the *New York Times* reporter: 'for a minute every eye shifted to the young woman at the defence table in the flowing black skirt and the black boots.' Carolyn's stepmother stood firm, however; black, she maintained, was not among Carolyn's favourite shades. 'She looks very good in bright colours.'

After the last echoes of the glove controversy died down, the balance of the defence's evidence seemed humdrum by comparison. A firearms expert, Jerold Steinberg, asserted that the silencer that machinist George Peters had supposedly made for Vincent Parco would not have functioned well enough for use in a shooting. Aronwald called a Bedford school secretary in a final effort to refute nurse January's belated recollection that, after finishing a conversation on the school's telephone, Carolyn Warmus had told the nurse that she had purchased a gun. The secretary described a telephone log in which teachers were asked to write down any private calls for later billing. There were no listings of any calls by Carolyn Warmus on the date of the conversation reported by nurse January. Aronwald suggested that this detail was a sufficient ground for the jurors to conclude that the nurse had made up the entire story.

Since Warmus's questionable telephone bill could not be introduced in evidence, the defence was compelled to take a fresh approach to the disputed call from Warmus's apartment to the gun shop. Aronwald summoned to the stand a private investigator, who said that it was possible for someone to have 'tapped' into Warmus's apartment line and made the call without her knowledge.

In his closing argument on 19 May, Aronwald argued that the victim, Betty Jeanne Solomon, was 'unwanted baggage' to her husband Paul and that he, not Carolyn Warmus, had the motive and the opportunity to kill his wife to clear the way for a series of love affairs. Aronwald strongly urged the jury to reject the wondrously materializing woollen glove. This was the evidence, he argued, that the prosecution hoped would swing the second jury in its favour. It was no accident, in Aronwald's view, that Solomon claimed to have discovered in his apartment the glove that the police had photographed next to his dead wife's body in January 1989 and then had lost. That glove, he reminded the jurors, was tested at the time and did not appear to have blood on it just after the murder. It was no accident either that now, according to prosecution witnesses, the glove was bloodstained, for it was Mr Solomon himself who had placed the blood there to try to link Carolyn Warmus to the murder scene.

Replying for the state, Assistant District Attorney McCarty urged that there was too much evidence tying Carolyn Warmus to the shooting to be explained away. 'These aren't a series of coincidences, ladies and gentlemen,' he said. 'Sooner or later the picture should become clear to you: you can see Carolyn Warmus doing this.' He argued that Paul Solomon had nothing to gain from the death of his wife and that only Warmus could have killed the woman she had come to view as an obstacle. Warmus's telephone bill showed that, on the day of the murder, she had called Solomon and talked to him for 55 minutes. During that call, she had learned that the Solomons' daughter was away for the weekend and that

Betty Jeanne would be alone. When Solomon told her that he had accompanied his wife to a bar mitzvah the day before, it was brought home to Warmus once again that she was on the 'bad side of a lovers' triangle'. In the course of the conversation she had made plans to meet Solomon at 7.30 that night at the Holiday Inn, and thirty minutes after the conversation ended, her phone bill showed the call to the New Jersey gunshop. The police placed Mrs Solomon's death at around 7.15 that night; the prosecutor reminded jurors that one witness at the Holiday Inn restaurant said that Solomon had arrived there at 7.30 and Warmus only later. In greeting Solomon, the prosecutor said, Carolyn had explained that she had been caught in traffic. 'Traffic,' McCarty repeated to the jurors with an expression of disbelief, '– on a Sunday night?'

After seven days of deliberations, the jury found Warmus guilty of second degree murder and illegal gun possession. Among the jurors, the black glove was the most frequently cited reason for the verdict. William Aronwald said: 'I have no doubt in my mind that without the glove the prosecution would not have hoped for anything better than a hung jury. It really derailed our defence.' David Lewis, defence lawyer at the first trial, was not reluctant to second-guess his successor, suggesting that Aronwald might have been hurt by moving away from a strategy of claiming more centrally that Warmus had been framed by Solomon and Parco:

> I think what we did in the first trial was to address the issue of a frame-up from the first meeting with the jury. That is, as far as I'm concerned, the major difference between the two trials.

In a decision announced on 26 June 1992, Judge Carey passed sentence on Carolyn Warmus. Belying the prosecution's persistent charges that he had a soft heart for the defence, Carey doubted neither the justice of the jury's verdict nor the gravity of the risk that

118

Warmus might repeat the criminal acts of which she had been convicted. Characterizing Warmus as a woman who 'unhesitatingly took another's life for no apparent purpose but that of having the victim's husband to herself,' the judge considered that the assurance of a long incarceration was necessary for the benefit of anyone who might anger her in the future as well as for those persons she might consider to have contributed to her conviction or to have harmed her in some other fashion. Operating under statutory sentencing guidelines, Carey defined his task as prolonging the time within which Warmus's adversaries, such as Paul Solomon and Vincent Parco, could 'sleep somewhat more soundly'. Any speculation, however, that the defendant might threaten a broader circle of the public 'would fly in the face of her non-violent career up to the time she brought herself under the evil influence of Vincent Parco, whose respect for the law is minimal.' Weighing these considerations, Judge Carey imposed a murder sentence of imprisonment for a term of not less than twenty-five years and a concurrent sentence under the gun possession count of confinement for not less than five years nor more than fifteen.

Even before the jury returned in her second trial, Carolyn Warmus had condemned herself to a more durable penance. In a courtroom conversation with a *Newsday* reporter, she vowed that she was finished with married men for all time.

AFTERWORD

On 15 March 1993, Carolyn Warmus's attorney filed a motion for a new trial, claiming that two pieces of key evidence had been withheld by the prosecution. Aronwald asserted that the prosecution knew that Paul Solomon had been having an affair with another woman, Barbara Ballor, three months *before* his wife was killed, and not four months *after* the murder, as he had testified. Moreover, the defence counsel asserted, the prosecution

119

had not disclosed to the jury the existence of a *second* glove, apparently found outside the Greenburgh apartment building; Aronwald contended that the prosecution had used the first glove to link Warmus to the slaying, but that the second would have acquitted her. Well, perhaps . . .

Running Commentaries

1

THE VILLAGE OF MAMHILAD is tucked away, a mile or so
west of the road between Pontypool and Abergavenny in
south Wales. Rather than lending prettiness to Mamhilad,
two streams running close by only emphasize the plain-
ness of the place; but still, far less because of its genteel
seclusion than because there is a golf club within strolling
distance, via a bridge over one of the streams, property
prices in Mamhilad are very high indeed. Take, for
instance, the medium-sized house just along the road
from the village pub, the Horseshoe: painted white and
standing on a shelf of land, and therefore called White
Crest, it would lack distinction but for some tarting-up of
the frontage – the gabling of three (strangely, not all four)
of the upstairs windows, the addition of an end-to-end
slated porch supported by brick-faced pillars. And yet,
in November 1992, when the likelihood that the house
would be put up for sale became a certainty, estate agents
touting for the job spoke of an ONO-less asking-price in
the region of a quarter of a million pounds.

Till six months before, White Crest had been the
home of the Horbury family: Peter, a stockily-built,
grey-haired man of fifty-five, his wife Caroline, who
was eight years younger, a former nurse, and their
ten-year-old son Daniel, a friendly, clever child, slim
and quite tall for his age, who, like his father, needed to
wear spectacles. The Horburys also owned a high-priced
flat in the part of London that is now known as Little
Venice. Handy for Paddington Station, the terminus for
trains from south Wales, the flat was used mostly by
Peter Horbury, who, being a consultant engineer, a

very successful one, was often in London for meetings with clients. As well as those short times away from Mamhilad, he was sometimes absent for weeks, even months, conducting assignments in foreign countries, particularly of the Middle East.

It seems that the absences made his heart grow fonder towards his wife and son. His love for Caroline, complete since he had courted her, had in recent years become tinged with a sort of gratitude; speaking about her to friends, of his alone or of both of them, he extolled her loyalty to him, said that he would be lost without her. Perhaps he had in mind the fact that medicine he had taken, still took, to reduce high blood-pressure had made him sexually impotent.

He doted on his son. Whenever he returned from an overseas trip, and often when he had only been away for a few days in London, he brought Daniel a present – lately, usually something to do with the boy's computer, itself a present from him the Christmas before last. In the garage, shrouded so as to protect its silver-coloured paintwork, was a so-called 'classic' sports car, an Alfa-Romeo Spyder, valued at £20,000, which he had bought to be his son's seventeenth-birthday present. That very special present for an unspecial birthday would be the last birthday present from Peter Horbury to his son that Daniel could not buy for himself, for on his next birthday, marking the start of his manhood, he would receive a bequest of a million pounds from his mother's parents, who were rich landowners.

Speaking only in terms of cash and kind, the Horburys – both as a family and as individuals, Peter, Caroline and Daniel – could count their blessings and look forward to the future with entire confidence.

Though Daniel was allowed to stay up later than his usual bedtime when he didn't have to go to school the next day, it was rare on such nights for neither of his parents to come up to his room at around ten to insist, if he wasn't already asleep, that it was time for lights-out. Till the night of Friday, 5 June 1992, he had never been allowed to stay up as late as half-past eleven. That was the time now, he saw by the clock on his video machine. He had been sitting on his bed, in his pyjamas, for a long while, since soon after his father had come back from the Horseshoe, since his parents had started arguing. They were in the living room; one of them had closed the door, had slammed it shut, and so he could not hear what the argument was about; he knew that it involved him in some way, because once or twice he had heard his name being shouted. There had been several arguments between them during the past week, following his father's return from an overseas trip, but none of those had been as loud or lasted as long. Early that morning, he had gone into their room, had seen that his mother was alone in their bed; wondering where his father could be, he had looked in the spare room and found him lying on the bed, wide awake. He wished to goodness he knew what the trouble was, in what way he was involved. Perhaps tomorrow he would ask them to tell him.

Suddenly the arguing stopped. He heard the living-room door open, then his mother's footsteps on the stairs. He quickly got into bed. When she came in to turn the light off, he would pretend to be asleep; he didn't want her to know that he had listened to the noise of the argument. Through the half-open door, he saw her crossing the landing to the bathroom. She had bathed while his father was at the pub, and was wearing her blue silk dressing-gown over her nightdress. She was cleaning her teeth.

His father came upstairs.

Daniel subsequently said: 'My dad went into the bathroom. He was asking her, "Do you still love me?" He was really cross – very, very cross. Then the door was closed. I heard a wallop and went into the bathroom. She was being strangled. His hands were on her neck and he was squeezing. I pulled him off, but he pushed me out of the room. He bolted the door. I shouted that I was going to call the police.'

There was a phone on a console table near the top of

the stairs. He picked up the receiver and pressed the 9 button three times. An operator asked him which emergency service he required. 'My mum and dad are fighting,' he said. 'Put me through to the police.' The call was automatically being recorded; electronics experts would be able to clarify background noises on the tape.

He told the operator his phone number, and when a constable at the local police headquarters came on the line, gave him the address. Still speaking to the constable, Michael Brown, he said: 'I don't know what is going on. There is a terrible row. They are fighting.' His voice became a scream: 'Come here – come here soon. Help. They are killing each other.'

> *Constable*: Listen to me. The police are on their way. They are on their way.
> *Daniel*: Please help. You've got to.

His father ran past him and down the stairs to the kitchen. When he ran back up the stairs, he was holding a carving knife. Daniel dropped the receiver and tried to hold on to him, but he pulled away and went back into the bathroom, leaving the door open.

The tape picked up a woman's voice: 'Please, please don't stab me, please . . .' A second later, there were loud cries.

Daniel picked up the receiver. 'Can you get an ambulance to come?'

> *Operator*: Calm down. We will tell them now.
> *Daniel*: My mum and dad are fighting. They are killing themselves.
> *Ambulance officer*: Where are you?
> *Daniel (screaming)*: My parents are distressed. Come quickly.
> *Operator*: They are on their way.
> *Daniel*: Thank you – you've helped me such a lot. I'm frightened to death. They are fighting. I hope my mum's not going to die. She's –

At that moment, his father emerged from the bathroom.

He did not have the knife.

Daniel said: 'Dad, have you killed her? You have done enough to me and my mum. You are not going to do any more. Have you killed her?'

'No,' his father replied.

'You better not have.'

His father said something in a low voice, too low for the tape to pick it up, and Daniel said, 'No – only if you promise that you won't go in there again.'

'Come here. I won't do it again.'

Peter Horbury took the receiver from his son and spoke to the operator, who told him that the police and an ambulance would soon be there. 'Yes, that's OK,' he said quietly.

By then, Daniel had gone into the bathroom. His mother's body lay across the tiled floor. Ragged cuts on the palms of her hands showed that she had at first tried to wrest the knife from her husband. He had stabbed her five times in the back before plunging the knife into her neck, leaving it there. Daniel subsequently said: 'I tried to give her the kiss of life. Then I looked at her, and I knew. I pulled the knife out slightly, but I knew she was dead.'

The boy ran from the bathroom. His father held out his hands to him, but he ran past, down the stairs and out of the house. He would never go back. Minutes later, police cars and an ambulance arrived. An ambulance man found Daniel near the garage: 'He was frantic – shouting and running around.'

He and his father were taken, in separate cars, to the police station at Pontypool. Daniel was kept there only until arrangements were made for him to be looked after by his mother's sister, who lived in a nearby village.

In November, Peter Horbury stood trial at Cardiff Crown Court. He admitted that he had killed his wife but denied the charge of murder, pleading provocation. Giving evidence in his own defence, he said that relations between himself and Caroline had become increasingly strained following his return from his last engineering assignment in the Middle East. He had accused her of having an affair while he was away. On the Thursday night, she had refused to let him sleep with her. The following afternoon, when he had got back to the house after a long walk, she had asked him where he had been. 'I replied, "It's not where I've been, but where you've been." I was being sarcastic, and she exploded. She hit me with both fists, knocking my spectacles off. She was shouting and screaming that she wanted out.' That night, after his visit to the pub, they had had a worse argument; following her up to the bathroom, he had again accused her of adultery, and she had said that it was true – that she intended to leave him, taking Daniel with her. 'I said to her, quite forcefully, "You are not taking Daniel anywhere."

'Then she turned around and said to me: "Why? He is not your child."

'When she said that, I just lost control. I hit her. I put my hands around her throat. I hit her again and again. I got the knife. Daniel tried to stop me, but I threw him aside. Then I stabbed Caroline. I cannot tell you how many times. The next thing I can remember is hearing Daniel's screams and going looking for him.'

In his first statement to the police, he had said: 'I am sure Daniel will never forgive me for what I have done, but still I hope he does.'

Daniel had told the police: 'My mum was a very nice person. She did everything for me. She stayed in with me every night. I loved her. I loved them both. I was very happy.'

The enhanced recording of the phone call was played to the jury, who later watched on closed-circuit television as Daniel, in another court, answered questions from both leading counsel.

The judge, Mr Justice Pill, summed up in the afternoon of Friday, 13 November, the fifth day of the trial. As the jury had not agreed on the verdict by the end of that day, they were lodged in a hotel overnight. Next morning, having continued their discussion for less than a hour, they decided unanimously that Peter Horbury was guilty of murder.

In passing the sentence of life imprisonment, the judge said that he had found no merit in the plea of provocation: 'Mrs Horbury was a good wife and a good mother. The suggestions made about her conduct were unacceptable and entirely without foundation.'

No doubt that was true; but did the judge mean that Peter Horbury had had no reason for being provoked by what (according to his uncontradicted testimony) his wife had said to him, simply because she had *lied* that she was an adulteress, that Daniel was not his son? Surely not.

Since September, Daniel had been at a boarding school, where he was registered under an assumed name; he had told classmates that his parents, both of them, were dead, victims of a motoring accident. The day after the trial, a tabloid published an article by a pair of sob-sisters, SECRET NEW LIFE FOR 'ORPHAN' OF MURDER, which revealed those facts. Making double sure that the boy's new life was no longer secret, a photograph of him filled one side of the half-page.

Another paper, not of the sleazy sort, quoted his aunt, his mother's sister, as saying that he never wanted to see his father again.

One hopes, as much for his sake as for his father's, that he will change his mind.

2

THOUGH PUKEKOHE IS BARELY large enough to be called a town, and though it lies fifty miles from the capital of New Zealand, Auckland, it is the nearest noticeable collection of buildings to the south of that city. The low land around Pukekohe, bounded on the northern side by a large bay, and bisected to the south by the Waikato River, is patched with farms, most of them growing potatoes. Few of the farmhouses are within sight of others. Among the exceptions are three houses that, till May 1992, were the homes of different members of the Schlaepfer family – descendants, like many other families in the area, of people who emigrated from Switzerland during the last decade or so of the nineteenth century.

At about eight o'clock on the morning of 20 May, a Wednesday, an emergency phone-call was put through to the police station in Pukekohe. The call was answered by a constable named Jeff Stuck, a lanky young man, dark and heavily moustached. He heard a woman's voice. It was high-pitched, close to shrieking. Little of what the woman said was coherent, but he had no difficulty in making out the words 'shootings' and 'family'. For a moment, the voice rose even higher, but it was, strangely, quieter, as if the woman were telling a terrifying secret that no one else should hear. Then the constable heard – flinched at – an explosion. Then he heard, overlapping the explosion, the sound of something or someone falling. Then he heard *tap* . . . *tap* . . . *tap* . . . *tap*, each of the sounds quieter, each of them separated by a longer silence, and he knew that he was hearing the phone swinging from its wire, tapping against a wall or a piece of furniture. He *knew* that the woman could no longer hear him. He shouted questions to her. And then, knowing that he would hear nothing more over the line, he kept his receiver tight against his ear, listening intently to the dead silence –

and, all of a sudden, heard a voice, a different voice, that of a child, a little girl, telling him that her name was Linda – Linda Schlaepfer. He learned later – some hours later – that she was nine.

He prompted her to say where she was speaking from, what had happened, what was happening – gathered that somebody was 'on the rampage, shooting at anyone he saw'. He had by now switched on the recorder attached to his phone. While continuing the conversation with Linda, he used another phone to send a message, the equivalent of an air-force 'scramble', to the police Armed Offenders Squad.

Afterwards, having sorted parts of the jumbled conversation into a sensible sequence, he recalled: 'The first Linda knew of the incident was when she heard a heated argument inside the farm-house earlier in the morning. Her mother yelled at her and her eleven-year-old brother Aaron to get back to bed. Aaron ran to his room, next to hers. She jumped back into bed and heard what she thought was a shot. She heard her mother yelling and then another shot and then her grandfather yelling for her. She told me: 'My grandad, he's shot my brother. I heard him go into Aaron's room. Aaron begged grandad not to kill him. I heard a shot. I hid in my wardrobe so he wouldn't shoot me. Then I heard mum say, "I don't know where Linda is."'

From the recording:

Constable: Where is your grandad now? Is he outside?

Linda: I don't know. I think he's coming back to shoot – he's going to shoot me. He's probably just here.

Constable: He's probably –

Linda: Probably looking for me.

Constable: Either looking for your mum or looking for you . . . Has your grandad still got the gun? Is it a rifle or is it a little gun or what?

Linda: It's a big one.

Constable: Can you tell me how this all started? Was it an argument?

Linda: I don't know. He just started shooting into the ground.

Constable: But who did he shoot first?

Linda: I don't know. Oh, my brother Aaron, then mum. My brother is bleeding all over. He's groaning – twitching.

Constable: Where's your grandad now?

Linda: He may be out looking for my dad, who's out on the farm – he's out picking. I heard grandad shout that he was going to look for dad.

The constable told her to lock all the outside doors. She

129

returned to the phone. She said: 'He's shot my mother, you know.'

>*Constable*: Where is your mother?
>
>*Linda*: Right beside me. I'll just see if she's still breathing.
>
>*Constable*: Is she all right?
>
>*Linda*: Can you come here immediately . . . hmmm?
>
>*Constable*: Policemen are on the way, Linda. What's happened to your mother?
>
>*Linda*: He shot her up the nose. She's just lying here.
>
>*Constable*: He shot her in the face?
>
>*Linda*: Yes . . . I think I know why he is shooting everyone. He's been having problems lately, and he's getting old. He's – he's been weird lately.

Realizing that Linda was becoming more distressed, the constable asked her if there was a phone she could use in her bedroom. She said that there was. He told her to go to her room, speak to him as soon as she got there, and then lock the door and push a chair under the knob. He afterwards recalled: 'Then I just kept her talking – about school and her interests, normal things like that. We even had a few laughs occasionally. She was very concerned about her three cats that hadn't had breakfast, and I had to assure her that the police would be feeding them. We could both hear noises in the downstairs part of the house. It may have been the cats. I knew by then that the police were outside the house but not yet in a position to enter the house. She said that it would be best if the police came in through a laundry door. I told her we would have to choose a signal-word for her to shout to the police, and we decided on 'rabbit'.

The constable's 'harrowing experience' came to an end when he heard sounds, including muffled voices, and Linda calling out: 'Rabbits, rabbits.' Then a policeman asking, 'Are you OK?' – and Linda, in a remarkably calm tone, saying, 'Yip.' She came back to the phone to tell Constable Stuck that she was safe and to say goodbye.

The police had already seen the dead bodies of her mother and her brother. During the next couple of hours, a search of another Schlaepfer farm-house and of nearby fields revealed the dead bodies of the grand-father's wife and his three sons, including Linda's father. The dead body of the grandfather, sixty-four-year-old Brian Schlaepfer, was found last of all, at three in the afternoon, in an outlying field; his index finger was still curled around the trigger of the shotgun that lay beside him.

The killings at Pukekohe constituted the second case of what might be termed rampage murders in New Zealand in just over eighteen months.

On the morning of Tuesday, 13 November 1990, David Gray, a thirty-three-year-old drug-addicted 'gun freak', had an argument with his neighbours in the seaside village of Aramoana, near Dunedin, on the South Island. He set their house alight, and when firemen arrived, appeared in the doorway of his own small house, where he had lived alone since the death of his mother a few years before. He was wearing, as he often did, camou-flaged battle-gear, and was carrying two semi-automatic rifles of the AK-47 type. He started shooting, at the same time screaming oaths at the firemen, who dived for cover, along with spectators and the people who had escaped from the burning house. Two children were wounded. He then roamed through the village, shooting at anyone he happened to see and entering houses in search of further targets. Shortly before a squad of armed policemen arrived, he went into hiding. He had killed thirteen people and seriously wounded several others. Among the dead were a boy of five and the village constable, a schoolfriend of Gray's, who had tried to persuade him to give himself up. The search for Gray continued through the night. Shortly after dawn, he was cornered near his home. Ignoring calls to surrender, he opened fire on the police, who, returning the fire, killed him.

Later that day, two gun-dealers, one in Christchurch, the other in Wellington, said that he had recently written to them, asking the prices of ammunition and parts for AK-47 rifles. The dealer in Christchurch said that the letter he had received 'could, on reflection, have been from an unstable person'.

So as not to leave the impression that murder is commonplace in New Zealand, I must mention that the number of murders known to the police in 1987 was 39; in 1988, 30; in 1989, 21; and in 1990, the year of the slaughter at Aramoana, 33.

A Lout Mission

WITH REFERENCE TO MAINLAND Britain, the vast majority of implements, blunt or sharp, used as murder weapons were intended by their makers for perfectly lawful purposes.

I am not changing the subject in saying that Mark Paul is a baseball fan; indeed, till the late summer of 1991, his keenness extended to playing that game most Sundays in parks in south London. It appears that, when the English soccer season came round, he would put away all but one item of his baseball gear, and revert to the sporting exercise of hooliganism, in common with other 'boot boys' who pretend support of Chelsea Football Club as a lame excuse for mob-violence.

He seems to have been something of a Jekyll-and-Hyde, for during the working day he was polite, nattily dressed, and with his wavy dark hair always carefully combed, and dainty in his handling of the pretty and delicate wares of the jewellery shop in Docklands where he was employed – just promoted, at the age of twenty-one, to the position of assistant manager, which suggests that his boss considered him law-abiding as well as reliable and bright. The manager was not aware that Mark Paul had been expelled from school; nor that he had been convicted of using threatening words and behaviour, of beating up the owner of a car he had tried to steal, and of assaulting a bus-conductor – at first with his fists, and then, having torn the man's ticket-machine from his shoulder, with that.

On the night of Tuesday, 3 September 1991 (an anniversary of the start of the Second World War), Paul made the awkward journey from Docklands to Battersea – to his home in Granfield Street, which, no more than

133

a hundred yards long, is tucked away behind the High Street, close to the Thames. He changed into casual clothes before going out with two friends. The name of one of the friends does not concern us. The other friend was Andrew Christie, who was Paul's flatmate.

I don't know whether Christie was as keen on baseball as Paul was; for all I know, he was not at all interested in the game. But when they left the flat, Christie carried Paul's bat – not visibly but surely making a noticeable bulge where it was stowed inside his lumber-jacket, for baseball bats are three feet long and thick as a rolling pin at the striking end.

The three friends strolled across Battersea Bridge to the King's Road, Chelsea, where they stayed till midnight, for most of the time drinking Australian-style lager in a pub or pubs. Speaking as a moderate drinker of real ale, I consider that even a sip of lager is too much; and so I find it hard to believe that anyone could stomach six pints of the stuff, as each of the three friends did. While drinking, Paul – I don't know about the others – smoked cannabis cigarettes.

The friend I have not named went home. Paul and Christie continued along the High Street, away from where they lived. Christie was now overtly carrying the baseball bat: sometimes swinging it, and occasionally, perhaps without meaning to, clouting fences, shop-doors, and at least one car-windscreen; Paul doesn't seem to have complained at the risk of damage to his sporting property. They met a young man, Tom Freud, a neighbour of theirs in Granfield Street. Though he took care to stay well over a swinging bat's length away from them, and was all the while poised to run, he distinctly heard Paul say that they were 'going to look for someone who had caused trouble'. Freud slipped away.

A short time later, probably no more than a few minutes, they spotted a man, John Lavender, walking towards them. He was a native of Birmingham, tall but of slender build; though he was only twenty-eight, his dark hair was sparse and receding from his forehead. He had recently gained a degree in business administration from the City of London University, to add to an honours degree in history from Jesus College, Oxford. Having spent the evening in Croydon with a woman he had once worked with, he was walking from Clapham Junction Station towards his flat in Sunbury Lane, a block or so from Granfield Street. Neither Paul nor Christie knew him, not even by sight; there is no indication that he had ever seen either of them.

They did not speak to him now. If Paul had not already retrieved his bat, he did so as John Lavender passed them, walking near the edge of the pavement. Holding the bat in both hands, Paul swung it at the back of the stranger's head, felling him. Then he and Christie ran home.

Both were asleep, and sleeping soundly, when, perhaps an hour later, three youths walking along the High Street noticed a small clump glistening near a lamp-post. The clump was of hair overladen with blood. Smeared gouts of blood extended to an alley, within which John Lavender was lying, his arms curled around his head as if to protect it; he was barely conscious, mumbling sounds, not words; his body was shaking all the time, often violently from convulsions.

It is good to know that, while one of the youths went for assistance, the others stayed with John Lavender, trying to comfort him.

He died in hospital in the early afternoon of the following day. One of the doctors who tended him said that he had never before seen such severe and extensive brain lacerations; 'the skull was split into several pieces'.

Paul knew the name of the man he had attacked, and knew that he was dead, before getting home from work, having seen a report in the *Evening Standard*. He and Christie talked of what had happened, but neither considered going to the police. On Sunday, Paul played baseball in Battersea Park, using the murder weapon when it was his turn to bat –

– or so he said a couple of days later, after he and Christie had been arrested as the result of a tip-off from someone whose identity, though not divulged by the police, seems apparent. Paul subsequently insisted that he had not played in the game, only watched from a side-line 'because of the bat . . . I didn't want to touch it.'

He did not argue with any other part of the police account of the interview: he at first claimed that he and Christie had gone straight home from the King's Road – but having been told that there was evidence to the contrary, admitted the crime, saying that he was 'completely unable' to explain why he had 'given the man a little tap on the head'. He said that he and Christie had not gone out that night with the intention of attacking anyone – 'we meant to do just criminal damage, just cars.' Told that Christie, already interviewed, had said that, on their return to Battersea, they had 'gone looking for trouble,' adding that they were on 'a lout mission' (a term used by Chelsea soccer hooligans), Paul agreed that that was 'about right'. He explained: 'When I mix cannabis with lager, it has more effect than when I take them separately, and that night I felt excited. I felt tipsy. I was in high spirits.' He said that he had not meant to kill, not even to cause serious injury to, the man he had since learned was John Lavender.

But when he appeared at the Old Bailey, exactly a year after the crime, the prosecution refused to accept his plea of Guilty to Manslaughter. Possibly from remorse rather than fear, he sobbed for long periods during the three-day trial – during the whole time he was in the witness-box – and particularly loudly when the jury, having been absent for five hours, convicted him of murder by an 11–1 majority, and while the judge, Mr Justice Hobhouse, spoke of his 'appalling crime' and sentenced him to life imprisonment.

John Lavender's mother afterwards commented: 'I hope he keeps on crying for the rest of his life. I can't forgive him: nothing excuses his crime, the fact that he left my son to die, didn't even call an ambulance. Paul committed murder simply because there was a head in front of him. It didn't matter whose head it was.'

You will have wondered what happened to Andrew Christie. He was brought to the Old Bailey a few days after the trial of his friend, and, having admitted conspiracy to cause criminal damage, was sentenced by Mr Justice Hobhouse to four and a half months' imprisonment. However, as he had spent longer than that in custody while on remand, he was immediately allowed to walk free.

A Dose of Death

LILLIAN BOYES, A WIDOW of the Hampshire village of Bishopstoke, suffered dreadfully from rheumatoid arthritis. With no disrespect to doctors who described her condition, I prefer to quote the Reverend Robert Clarke, a chaplain at the Royal Hampshire County Hospital, Winchester, who visited her frequently during each of the many times when she was a patient on the St Cross ward, latterly only to receive drugs that either partly controlled her disease or slightly and briefly eased her suffering:

'Apart from the neck up, where her brain was very bright, her whole body was wracked with pain. I have seen young children awaiting bone-marrow transplants, people dying of cancer, and people blown apart by the IRA, but I don't think I have ever, ever seen a patient who was so degenerate physically, so eaten into by disease, so pain-ridden in such an accumulation of ways that it is impossible to list them. By August 1991, her arms were no thicker than my two middle fingers, and if touched, she would scream. When anyone touched her, even just lightly on the hand, you could hear the joints move. It was the most haunting sound and one I will probably take to the grave. Yet she seldom complained, was always cheerful, and was capable of holding a sensible and balanced conversation. Her sister Midge, who also suffered from rheumatoid arthritis, died in July, and Lillian said she hoped it would not be too long until she also would be free of pain.'

For the previous thirteen years, since 1978, she had been under the care of Dr Nigel Cox, a consultant rheumatologist at the hospital. He, at forty-six, was a roly-poly, pink-faced man, bespectacled, whose blond

138

hair had receded, making his forehead, which was only slightly wrinkled, appear very large. His manner, at any rate towards nursing staff, was brusque. He conducted his private practice at his home in the nearby village of Calden Common, where he had lived since the end of a marriage that had produced two sons, and where he often entertained a woman of his own age.

During Lillian Boyes's stay in the hospital in the summer of 1991, she told a junior doctor that she wanted to die, and asked if he could give her something to 'hasten death', which he said was not possible as he would run the risk of being charged with murder. By the start of August, not even heroin was easing her pain, and on the sixth, a Tuesday, in accordance with her wish, Dr Cox withdrew the drugs that were helping to control her condition; he ordered that she was to be given a one-milligram dose of diamorphine every hour to give her some slight relief. Over the next two days, the pain unexpectedly worsened, and he increased the dosage. On Friday morning, he gave her 100 mg of diamorphine together with diazepam, a sedative, thinking that she would die within an hour.

But she was still alive when her sons, John and Patrick, visited her in the afternoon. Dr Cox came to her bedside. He spoke to her and then left the ward. When he returned, he was holding a hypodermic syringe. After searching her frail body for a vein that had not collapsed, he injected her in a foot. She died within a few minutes. Patrick Boyes shook hands with Dr Cox and thanked him, either generally or for a particular act. Shortly afterwards, when Sister Roisin Hart came on duty, the body was being laid out. Dr Cox had left by then. On the death certificate he had completed, he had written 'R.I.P.'

Sister Hart detected a strange atmosphere among the nurses. Eventually, one of them told her to look at Dr Cox's notes on Lillian Boyes. The penultimate note showed that he had administered two ampoules of potassium chloride – a drug with no therapeutic or analgesic properties, one ampoule of which is likely to cause death.

'I was totally stunned,' Sister Hart afterwards said. 'The notes had been left at the nurse station for all to see. I didn't know what to do. Everyone on the shift knew what had happened, and they all seemed to be looking at me as if to say, "What happens now?" By documenting what he had done, Dr Cox had involved the nurses. It was so blatant. I knew we couldn't cover it up. I would have been an accessory if I had done so. The notes would go to audit, and it would come out then.

'But still, I was in a dilemma. I decided to give myself the weekend to think it over. I discussed it with my husband Ted [a nurse on the ward]. Early in the following week, I tried to speak to Dr Cox, but didn't have the opportunity. I don't find him the most approachable person.

'On the Wednesday, I decided I had to report what I had seen. It was a difficult decision as I knew some people would disagree with me. When I told my manager, I was sent to see the director of nursing services, and the police were called in.'

By then, the body of Lillian Boyes had been cremated.

According to the Crown Prosecution Service, that meant that – despite the close proximity in time between the injection and the death – there was insufficient evidence that the death had been caused by the injection of potassium chloride. Therefore, Dr Cox was charged with *attempted* murder. The hospital suspended his contract, but continued to pay him; he still treated private patients at his home.

It wasn't until more than a year later, in September 1992, that he stood trial at Winchester Crown Court. If verdicts were decided on the basis of a head-count of witnesses speaking respectively for the prosecution and the defence, he would have been entirely confident of acquittal. A host of witnesses – many of them doctors, but also including Lillian Boyes's sons – spoke up for him.

David Blake, Professor of Rheumatology at the Royal London Hospital, seems to have spoken from hearsay. He referred to the 'exquisite pain' Mrs Boyes must have felt as her primary illness grew worse, inflaming joints, deforming bones, and destroying tendons; also of complications, among them blood-poisoning and anaemia (both heightening the pain), bleeding in the stomach, a liver complaint which led to 'catastrophic bleeding' in the oesophagus and gullet, and sinus problems, resulting in multiple sores which penetrated the bones, weakening them to such an extent that they caused a crush-fracture of the spine. He spoke of the 'extraordinary dilemma' for Dr Cox, with a patient who was not responding to heroin as a pain-killer and whose brain refused to give up. Asked by the judge, Mr Justice Ognall, what options Dr Cox had, the professor said: 'One option was to do nothing more than give Mrs Boyes a cuddle. The consequence of that caring gesture would have been immediately to reduce her blood-pressure so that she would have died after a few seconds. When you are practising medicine for the care of the dying, you are struggling with dignity and decent human behaviour. Dr Cox could easily have walked away; but that, in my opinion, would have been a harm. In that situation, I don't think he did any harm.'

Dr Alan Dixon, a retired rheumatologist, said: 'I can only hope that I would have had the courage to do what Dr Cox did. I would have been ashamed of myself if I had not. The law leaves doctors in a very curious position. We are allowed to give drugs to relieve pain even though they shorten life. But at the same time we are not allowed to give drugs to shorten life even though they may alleviate pain. That is the razor's edge we are up against at the moment.' Dr Dixon said that it was 'absolutely proper' to use large doses of pain-killers to cut short the life of a person who was suffering and had no chance of recovering, and told of a time when, as a young doctor in China, he had helped the crew of a crashed aircraft: 'It was my duty to do what I could.

141

Several of the airmen died rapidly, but, with one, the only thing I could do was give vast doses of morphine through the cooked skin so that he died quickly and without pain.'

Several of Dr Cox's patients praised him, one, a retired nurse, saying that he had treated her for twelve years and that he was one of the most caring persons she knew.

Perhaps for a reason connected with something I shall mention in a moment, Sister Roisin Hart did not give evidence in person. A statement from her was read out in court.

In his closing address to the jury, the doctor's counsel, Sydney Kentridge, QC, quoted part of Dr Dixon's evidence, and went on: 'Your duty is to decide on which side of the "razor's edge" this case falls. All the testimony shows that the injection did relieve Mrs Boyes's suffering in the last moments. She was allowed to come to a peaceful, calm and dignified end – that is Dr Cox's alleged crime.' Describing the case as 'unprecedented in the history of our courts,' he appealed for an absolute discharge.

Neil Butterfield, QC, for the Crown, argued that the doctor had gone beyond his duty to care for his patient by giving her an injection with the purpose of killing her and ending her suffering. 'It was the defendant's duty to ensure that his terminally ill patient died with dignity and with as little suffering as possible. That was the full extent of his duty. Thus far and no further. We are not concerned with debating the difficult moral and philosophical questions of mercy-killing and euthanasia: this is a criminal trial. The whole ethos of the medical profession is to preserve life, and when that is no longer possible, to make life as peaceful as the condition of the patient permits. The dose of potassium chloride was double the lethal measure. The deliberate killing of a helpless person, whatever the wishes of that person and however terrible their pain, is not the right, nor the duty, of any doctor.'

Summing up on Friday, 18 September, the judge told the jury that they had listened to a 'sad and testing story' but that they had to 'set aside their emotions and consider the evidence objectively and impartially'. He said that Dr Cox, 'a distinguished professional man of unblemished reputation,' was alleged to have behaved in a way that was 'a clear repudiation of a doctor's lifelong duty, namely to save and not to take life. Honourable motives are no defence in this case. The deliberate taking of life by a doctor is as much against the law as in any other case.' Mr Justice Ognall said that there were a number of important factors for the jury to take into account: a strong bond had been formed between doctor and patient, which might help to explain why the injection was given; potassium chloride had no therapeutic or analgesic uses; patients sometimes confounded doctors by making recoveries that defied all expectations – 'which is, no doubt, one of the many reasons which explain why doctors are absolutely prohibited from taking life as opposed to saving it.'

The jury, sent out on the Friday afternoon, continued discussing the case next morning: for eight hours in all. When they returned, some of the women members were weeping. They had reached a majority-verdict, 11–1, that Dr Cox was guilty as charged. The judge delayed the sentencing till the Monday, when he told the doctor:

'What you did was not only criminal, it was a total betrayal of your unequivocal duty as a physician. It must be very clearly understood that such conduct can never be legally excused – though sometimes it can be explained. I have no doubt that this trial has been a terrible ordeal for you, and the verdict a personal and professional catastrophe. A message has to go from this court that your action was undoubtedly against the law. Because a patient died, there has to be a prison sentence as a matter of principle.'

The sentence was a year's imprisonment – suspended.

And so the doctor walked free. Outside the court, reunited with his girl-friend, he read a statement:

'Clearly, I am devastated by the verdict and the sentence for what was a bona fide act that was solely in the interests of Mrs Boyes. It seems somewhat harsh to criminalize me for doing my best in what were quite exceptional circumstances.

'Let us not forget Mrs Boyes, who was a brave and patient lady, and her family, who have been obliged to relive her end by proxy in the last ten days. I hope the press will now allow them to grieve in peace. I think that is the most important part of this statement. My aim now is to get back to a normal life as quickly as possible.'

He had received, and would continue to receive, scores of letters from well-wishers, several enclosing cheques, one for as much as £500. He paid the donations, eventually totalling more than £15,000, into a trust-fund in Lillian Boyes's name, the purpose of which was to aid research into rheumatoid arthritis.

During and after the trial, Sister Hart also received letters and phone calls from strangers. Most were anonymous, all were abusive, and some were threatening; one of the callers said that, with the nights drawing in, he would 'get her' in the hospital car-park. Already the mother of two children, she was in the seventh month of another pregnancy. Several of the signed letters were from zealot members of the Voluntary Euthanasia Society, and some of those writers gave the strong impression that they would be only too happy to conduct experimental mercy-killing on her. A number of writers and callers accused her of having 'informed on' Dr Cox for the simple reason that she was a Roman Catholic. She ignored advice that she should move to a secret address for the time being, and continued to work on the St Cross ward. In an interview, she said that she was disappointed that the United Kingdom Central Council for Nursing, the profession's disciplinary body, had not issued a statement supporting her action in revealing what Dr Cox had done: 'They could have used it as a chance to reinforce the code of conduct.'

She pointed out that it was made clear during the trial that a nursing sister who discovers an irregularity has no choice but to report it, and she went on:

'I think hospitals could learn from this case. I and my colleagues were told not to say anything to the media, but because of that I have ended up being a scapegoat. But I would do it over again if I had to. I just want the system changed, so that nurses faced with a similar dilemma can make the right decision without having to put up with the sort of persecution my family and I have been through.'

In November, Dr Cox travelled to London to give evidence before the General Medical Council's nine-member professional conduct committee. In seeking to explain and excuse his action, he said: 'I was faced with what seemed like several evils. I chose what seemed to be the least evil.' After an adjournment of more than four hours, the committee returned, and the chairman announced the decision: that although what Dr Cox had done was both unlawful and 'wholly outside a doctor's professional duty to a patient,' it was proposed that, in line with the trial-judge's 'tempering of justice with mercy, the case should be concluded' – there would be no disciplinary action. Dr Cox, who had feared that he would be struck off the medical register, sat down and buried his head in his hands.

A few days later, the Wessex Regional Health Authority said that he could return to work in the new year. With provisos, though: another consultant would for some time be his 'mentor', overseeing his actions; people attending his outpatient sessions at the hospital would have the choice, for at least a year, of seeing another doctor; he would be required to attend courses in pain-management; he would be required to meet staff members, to resolve 'frictions that had arisen'.

He returned to the hospital in February 1993, eighteen months after the sudden death of Lillian Boyes. Ambushed by reporters on his way in, he said that he did not expect hostility from staff or patients. What of his relations with Sister Hart? 'I shall be polite,' he murmured. 'I've no idea what her reaction will be.'

Getting Gotti Good!

JEFFREY BLOOMFIELD

AMERICA HAS ALWAYS PRIDED itself on its reputation as the 'land of opportunity', where poor immigrants find that 'the streets are paved with gold'. In fact, most immigrants find life a hard struggle, and live in the lower third of the economic spectrum for the first generation or so. How quickly they rise out of poverty and the ghettos depends largely on their racial and religious background. Currently, an immigrant from Latin America or Africa is more likely to be kept down than any from a European, Japanese, or Chinese heritage. But it was not always so easy for Europeans . . . at least, those from eastern or southern Europe. One of the groups that found it very hard to make a beachhead here were the Italians. In the first century of our existence as a nation, Italians were a curiosity and rarely seen, not even in major cities. But after Italy was unified in the 1860s, many Italians began coming to the US, hoping to find that promised land with the golden streets.

It is always very tricky talking about other peoples, because there is the danger that statements you make about them may sound bigoted. Therefore, let me say that Italians are hard-working, honest, and law-abiding people, who are *possibly* the most maligned in the world. The popular image, at least since the 1890s in the US, is that of wine-guzzling spaghetti-eaters, in garish clothing, who are oversexed, worship a faith that is full of obsolete superstitions and dogmas, and make a living in well-organized gangster mobs. That this image exists, despite the fact that Western society has derived

147

benefits from the Etruscan, Roman and Renaissance Ages that came from the Italian Peninsula, is due to hatred and envy directed at a whole group: a hatred that carefully picks out certain bad examples and ignores the conditions that enabled them to grow into being.

Because of the grinding poverty faced by Italians when they landed, and the really low-paid, humiliating jobs they had to take, *some* of them became criminals. The first criminal gangs preyed on the Italian immigrant communities themselves, levelling blackmail by threats of death or destruction of property. These gangs would often leave written threats which had a 'signature': an inked hand – hence the term 'Black Hand'. Initially, to the non-Italian public following the doings of these gangs in the yellow press, most of the crimes were ascribed to 'Black Handers'. However, a new term entered the lexicon in 1890. On 15 October of that year, David Hennessy, the Chief of Police of New Orleans, was shot to death in that city. Hennessy had made something of a career going after criminals of Italian background, even making international headlines in 1881 when he brought one back to the United States for trial. He was a man with many enemies, and not all the details of the events leading to his death are certain. However, he had been looking into the possible presence of Italian criminal gangs on the New Orleans waterfront. In the process, for the first time in American history, the term 'Mafia' for a Sicilian criminal organization was revealed. As Hennessy was dying, he told a friend that he had been shot by Italians. Eleven were arrested for the murder, but all were acquitted (possibly due to bribery and intimidation, though it must be said that much of the evidence against them was weak). On 14 March 1891, a mob of citizens lynched the Italians. The ensuing international furore led to a break in diplomatic relations between the US and Italy, until President Benjamin Harrison (after his own inquiry) paid an indemnity to the families of the dead Italians.

The original 'Mafia' had been set up to protect

native Sicilians from oppresive foreign invaders. Never disbanded, it gradually changed its character into an oppressive one. Like other secret societies, it has its own initiation rules, and lives on a code based on total respect for the entire body and membership (known as *la cosa nostra*). In theory, the members are pledged to respect each other in the hierarchy of the guiding families that have divided up the various territories. The foot soldiers owe allegiance to an immediate boss, the *consiglieri*, who owes allegiance to the *capo*, the head of the family.

But that is only the theory. It is inevitable, with so many violent men involved, that some of them are going to get tired of taking orders, and will want advancement. Also the heads of families might have expansion plans at each other's expense. Finally, every now and then the head of the largest mob in a city may feel entitled to the title of *capo di capo* – chief of chiefs. Some of the other mob leaders will resent this, and a bloody war can break out. One in New York City in 1930–1 only ended when junior mobsters killed the two mob leaders who were fighting for the title.

After that incident, the New York City area was 'straightened out' by gangsters 'Lucky' Luciano, Frank Costello, Albert Anastasia, and Vito Genovese. Taking their cue from big business, instead of cutting each other's throats, they formed a board-room type of arrangement, in which five Italian families ruled all the rackets. This set-up actually worked very well until the 1980s. Leaders of the families might change (Luciano was deported, Costello 'officially' retired, Genovese died in prison, and Anastasia was murdered), but the basic family units remained intact.

That is no longer the case, because of one man: Mr John Gotti. He achieved the title of *capo di capo*, but he may very well have destroyed the Mafia in the process.

John Gotti was born in 1941, the fifth of thirteen children of poor immigrants. His home was in the East

Harlem area of Manhattan, which was an Italian enclave then. It was a rough area, and Gotti became a tough street-fighter, as did some of his brothers. Although he was never interested in school, he had an IQ of 140. The family made several moves as he grew up, in the hope of finding a better life in another district. Unfortunately their moves were from one slum to another. Young Gotti continued fighting while at school, and learned other illegal activities in areas like the Brooklyn waterfront. Their final move was to the 'East New York' section of Brooklyn, which was notorious as the headquarters of Albert Anastasia's and Louis Lepke's 'Murder Inc.' Although that organization was broken up in 1943–4 (with the electrocution of Louis Lepke for murder – he was the only major crime boss ever executed in the USA), the area had many illegal gambling shops and other illegal activities going on. One more step in Gotti's education.

Gotti dropped out of school, joined a local gang, and by force of personality (including a violent temper), became its leader. At fifteen, he was running an illegal gambling operation. He got to know other young punks. One was Wilfred 'Willie Boy' Johnson, who became a close associate. A local Mafia 'soldier' noticed Gotti, and hired him to run errands. Thanks to his good memory, he was extremely efficient as a collector for local loan-sharks. Then he was arrested in 1957 for disorderly conduct. The charges were dropped, but the police had now noticed John Gotti.

He had moved into the gang of Carmine Fatico, in which he was an enforcer, a hijacker, and an occasional killer. The police were aware that Gotti had beaten up a salesman who had insulted Fatico, and who disappeared soon afterwards. No charges were brought in this 1967 incident, probably due to a lack of any evidence of a murder. It would not be the last occasion, nor the most notorious, that Gotti's name would be linked to that of a man who disappeared. Meanwhile, Fatico had moved his operations into the Ozone Park area of Queens, using the Bergin Hunt & Fish Club as his headquarters. Gotti and his criminal brothers were among the closest associates of their boss.

Since his first arrest in 1957 Gotti had been arrested many times, but no charge was ever successfully pursued. Then he and his brother Gene made a mistake: they were caught trying to steal $30,000 worth of electronic goods and women's clothes at JFK Airport with forged papers. In 1969 they were convicted and sent to Lewisburg Federal Prison in Pennsylvania. It was a four-year sentence, but Gotti got out on parole after three years. He had met many Mafiosi in the prison, and learned much about how the Mafia was organized. In particular, he had learned the inner workings of New York City's largest 'Family', that of Carlo Gambino.

When Gotti was released, he was put in charge of Fatico's gambling operations. This was somewhat ironic, for Gotti's biggest weakness (aside from power-hunger) was gambling. But because of his own weakness, he knew precisely how to batten on other gamblers. Gotti was also learning about business racketeering, the pornography business, and the fencing of stolen securities. One might think that he would have been satisfied with his success within the system, but he was ambitious to go right to the top of the mob family.

In January 1973, a son of Carlo Gambino was kidnapped. The kidnapper, one James McBratney, must have been remarkably stupid, because he took $100,000 and still killed the boy. Gotti was one of the men picked to punish McBratney. Actually they fumbled the job: they went to Staten Island to capture him, but he gave them trouble and one of them shot him dead. The police arrested Gotti. Gambino made some deal with the Staten Island District Attorney, and Gotti pleaded guilty and was given only four years for attempted manslaughter (he had not fired the gun). He spent this prison sentence at Green Haven, a New York prison, and was paroled again in 1977. Now he had paid his dues to the Mob, and in the summer he was formally inducted into the Mafia.

Because of later repercussions, I have to digress here about Mafia rules. I mentioned earlier the code of respect that is at the base of the organization's hierarchy. In practice, there is rivalry about who has control over what, but if the territories are clearly delineated by all the heads of the families, nobody dares to question their decision. Also, there is a rule of never raising a hand against a fellow member. Now this rule too has been broken in the past, but usually when the heads of the families have concluded that the fellow member has acted in such a way as to cease to merit the rule's protection. In 1957, Albert Anastasia, a founding member of the five families, had begun invading the territories of other members. He was given several 'friendly' warnings to abide by past agreements, but refused. He ended up being shot to death in a hotel barber-chair. That was a rare occasion. Normally, to avoid violence that was of no productive use, the Mafia favoured some kind of compromise. Carlo Gambino was a master of this type of diplomacy. But he died in 1976, one year before John Gotti was inducted into the organization.

Gambino's passing has an important symbolic value to this story. In 1931, when the five families were set up, the leaders were all first-generation Italian immigrants. So was Gambino. All had been born in Italy, and had some strong concept of respect for rules and hierarchy and honour. I know this may sound strange, for we are discussing murderous thugs, but that first generation valued their past, and were able to graft it with American business methods to make it work. But the generation of John Gotti, born in the United States from 1940 onwards, knew nothing of the sense of *noblesse oblige* which was part of the original Mafia's strength. It had tied the heads of families to their underbosses and soldiers with bonds of loyalty. Gotti and his generation would give lip-service to these ideals, so that the old mobsters would be pleased, and advance them – but once they were in the positions of real power, they would drop these ideals as so much useless baggage. What is more they would willingly turn on the old bosses.

After Gotti's first prison term was over, when Carmine Fatico put him in charge of the gambling operations, he was told that the Gambino Family frowned at money made in the drugs trade. Gotti nodded his head, as though the message was accepted, and then created a system where he could appear to have nothing to do with drugs, while his associate, Sal Ruggiero, did the dirty work. The mobsters above Gotti were taken in by this facade.

As a rising underboss in the Mob, Gotti moved to the Howard Beach area in Queens with his family (he had married Victoria DiGiorgio back in 1960, and they had two sons and two daughters). Here, despite his occasional displays of violent temper, he seemed to be finding an element of stability. His older son, John Jr, was a disappointment, being a violence-prone model of himself, but the younger one, Frank, was an intelligent boy, and the hope of his father in achieving a set of respectable, middle- or even upper-class heirs. Like many mobsters, Gotti yearned for his family to break free of their evil, poverty-stricken roots. Frank Gotti looked very promising, but on 18 March 1980, the boy was killed in a car accident.

If ever anybody was born under an unlucky star, that person was John Favara, a neighbour of the Gottis. Driving home that day, Favara had the sun in his eyes. Frank Gotti darted out from behind some garbage cans, and was hit by the car. Favara quickly learned how serious his position was: he attempted to pay his respects to Mrs Gotti, and apologize for the accident, only to be hit on the head by the lady with a bat. She began to goad her husband about letting their son's 'murderer' live, and erected a shrine in memory of Frank Gotti in the house. Actually, there was little need for her to press her husband, who was in a state of emotional anger far beyond his normal bad temper. Soon Favara's car was stolen. It was located wrecked, with the word 'murderer' written on it. His house was vandalized, and his mailbox found to contain a funeral card with a picture of the dead boy. There were furtive looks and whispers whenever he appeared. When he asked the police for protection, they said they couldn't give him any, and could not act against Gotti; they suggested that he should either kill Gotti or sell his home quickly and move out of the state. Favara had actually put his home up for sale when he was confronted by three men, knocked out, and driven away in a van. That was in May 1980. John Favara has never been seen since. Rumours of his fate are reminiscent of the film *The Texas Chainsaw Massacre*.

Tragic as is the destruction of this hapless man, one has to admit that the New York City Police happened to be right about their inability to help him. The only thing that could have been pushed was an assault charge against Victoria Gotti for hitting Favara with the bat, and no court would have been hard on her because she would have pleaded that she was distraught over her son's death. Nothing actually linked Gotti to the stealing and wrecking of the car, the vandalism, or the abduction. Common sense could find a connection, but common sense without evidence is worthless. The Favara incident was simply one more item for the police to add to their growing record of Gotti's career.

The regular course of business kept Gotti busy for the next few years, but meanwhile he was watching the changing shape of New York City's Mafia power. After Carlo Gambino's death, the press had pinpointed one Carmine Galante, a bald-headed old thug with a perpetual frown on his face, as the new chief mob boss in the city. Actually this was an exaggeration, though Galante would have liked to make it true. In 1979 it became a moot point, when Galante was gunned down while eating lunch at a Brooklyn restaurant. Now the man generally conceded as filling Carlo Gambino's shoes (if for no other reason, as head of the Gambino Crime Family) was Paul Castellano. Like Gambino, he was of the older generation, believing in the original sense of honour and respect for members that the Mafia stood for (in theory). Castellano was not as over-enthused about Gotti as other *consiglieri* were. He could sense the ruthless ambition and the lack of control in that young Turk.

Castellano never failed to watch Gotti and to look for any breach of Mafia rules. In 1981, he reiterated the ban on drug deals. Whether Castellano knew of Gotti's involvement at the time is not certain, but it is likely that he soon learned of it. As mentioned, Gotti had put his close friend, Sal Ruggiero, in charge of the drug business. Sal's brother Angelo was a party to all the secrets of the business, and unfortunately, he happened to talk too much. Castellano heard. He could not act quickly, as he had pressing legal difficulties with the government, but by 1985, having given a number of veiled warnings to Gotti, all ignored, he decided to arrange the execution of the latter. However, Gotti had been busy too, making a valuable alliance with Castellano's underboss, Frank DeCicco. Castellano had a conference with DeCicco on 14 December 1985, setting up arrangements for a meeting with Gotti at Stark's Steak House in Manhattan in two days' time. It seems likely that Castellano either hinted at or openly stated his intention to kill Gotti. No doubt, as a good friend, DeCicco told Gotti what was planned. On 16 December, Castellano was driven to Stark's by his chauffeur, Thomas Bilotti. Both were shot to death by assassins, waiting in a nearby car.

The police immediately suspected Gotti, though (again) they had little real evidence. Gotti spent the next year solidifying his control over the Gambino family, establishing his henchmen in the main positions of power. His success in that regard was not due to brilliant politics. Most of his opponents were old men who figured that acquiescence was the healthiest policy; they all wished to be allowed the chance to die in bed, not untidily in a street like Castellano. Had Gotti taken a moment to consider what his success was based on, he might have questioned how real it was. Not only was it based on the fear felt by a set of old men who would soon be dead or retired, but Gotti had just demonstrated that the head of the mob was a figure with feet of clay: if Castellano could be killed by Gotti the Young Turk, what was to prevent some other Young Turk from killing Gotti? Loyalty had protected the likes of Luciano, Costello, and Gambino – but Gotti, by his own actions, had shown the true value of loyalty among thugs and thieves. His throne was already insecure.

Soon afterwards, an unanticipated act should have tipped him off about the effect of his ambitious actions. As a reward for betraying Castellano, Frank DeCicco was made Gotti's underboss. In April 1986, DeCicco was blown up by a car-bomb. The killers were never caught, but it appears that they were hired by the family of Thomas Bilotti, the chauffeur-bodyguard murdered with Castellano. The killing shook Gotti's confidence in a way nothing had before.

It is very odd, when discussing mobsters in real life, how frequently the truth repeats the scripts of those old Hollywood crime films with Edward G. Robinson or James Cagney. Like the ancient morality stories, the start of a tale follows the central figure as he advances in material wealth and power, usually at the expense of society, and then reaches a high point: now he can go no further, and at this point the fates decree that he should begin the descent from power and prestige to disgrace. For John Gotti, the high point was the year 1986, when he replaced Paul Castellano as *capo di capo*. That year marked the start of the series of trials that was to end with him in a federal prison for life.

The destruction of John Gotti was started by a man he considered a friend. When Gotti began his street-gang career in the 1950s, one of his closest associates was Willie Boy Johnson. Gotti was unaware of it, but Johnson subsequently held a grudge against Carmine Fatico, Gotti's old patron: it seems that Johnson agreed to take the blame for an armed robbery, which entailed a three-year spell in prison, on the understanding that

Fatico would take care of Johnson's family; Fatico failed to do so, and Johnson came out of jail to find his wife and children on welfare. Johnson became an informant to the FBI and the Queens District Attorney's Office. How Gotti, with his sources and connections, never knew this until it was too late is one of the minor mysteries of the story. Not only did Gotti fail to latch on to Johnson's treachery, but he relied on the man to commit many important crimes for him: Johnson was one of the three men who abducted John Favara.

In 1987 the Queens District Attorney's office brought racketeering charges against Gotti and eight associates, including Johnson. Apparently, they hoped that Johnson would prove to be a fully cooperative witness, if faced with probable conviction; they also thought that the FBI would be glad to cooperate. They were wrong on both counts. The FBI has always been loathe to share information with state authorities, fearing that its operations will be compromised. As for Johnson, as the trial approached he was given reminders of the recent deaths of Castellano and Bilotti, making him fully aware that it would be distinctly unhealthy to testify against the new Boss of Bosses. Gotti hired Barry Slotnick, the famous defence attorney, to represent him. He also decided to maintain his public image, which this trial would soon enhance.

The old-time mob bosses had, for the most part, been very low-key in public. They did not court the eye of photographers; well-dressed and groomed, they looked like successful middle-class businessmen. The two glaring exceptions to this had been Al Capone and Bugsy Siegel, the former flaunting his power even for newsreels, the latter frequently getting his picture taken with show-biz stars. In both their cases, the public image did them harm: Capone looked as if he was too powerful, almost inviting another government trial; Siegel's spend-thrift methods of developing Las Vegas shook the confidence of his associates, forcing them to have him killed. But that was in an earlier time. In the 1980s, Gotti, with his thousand-dollar wardrobes, his swagger, his (for the public) smile, looked perfect for the media. He cultivated the image of a misunderstood nice guy: his press releases emphasized that every Fourth of July he put on a giant fireworks display for his neighbourhood; he could guarantee that a crowd of neighbours (many of them members of the Bergin Club) would come down to the courthouse and voice their disapproval of the legal 'persecution' of their beloved friend.

The Queens trial was a fiasco. One witness spoke of Gotti's bragging of murders and the planning of other crimes, but the witness was so unsavoury himself as to render his testimony worthless. A second witness, confronted by demands that he testify against the new head of organized crime, claimed that an assistant district attorney had offered sexual favours if he would lie about Gotti. Willie Boy Johnson's position would have been comical had it not been for the danger he faced. Though he kept denying that he was ever an informer, he was treated as a hostile witness, which meant that information that only he was privy to was produced in court: even if he demonstrated an unwillingness to tell the truth about Gotti, the latter was fully able to see what he had been up to. On Friday, 13 March 1987, the jury found Gotti and his fellow defendants not guilty. In August 1988, Willie Boy Johnson was shot to death. When informed of the 'mysterious' death of his one-time friend, Gotti said, 'Well, we've all got to go sometime.'

The 1980s was the period of the Presidency of Ronald Reagan. It was called the 'Teflon Presidency' because the President was so well liked that, no matter what scandals arose, he maintained his 'clean' fatherly image. Gotti, with his rapid advance to supreme power in the New York City Mob, and now his acquittal on a serious legal charge, became the 'Teflon Don'. It looked as if nothing could or would ever be successfully laid against him. Judging from his confident mien, his arrogant comments, he began to believe this nonsense himself.

And it is here that the real controversy of the case of John Gotti appears for the first time. As we read of his career, we are aware that (*1*) the *evidence* needed to convince any jury of his guilt was woefully non-existent; and (*2*) the sordid *details* were there, to convince any rational person that he was as evil and guilty as the state and federal governments claimed. Despite his pleasing public persona, his 'good neighbour policy' in Howard Beach (*pace* Mr Favara), he was not a desirable person to have out in society. With every successful evasion of a legal charge, Gotti was defying the government. No government will suffer such treatment indefinitely, since to do so renders it contemptible in the eyes of the public. Whether, had his operations occurred during a period of national domination by the Democratic Party, he would have found his successes more easily 'stomached', is an interesting question. As it was, Gotti's misfortune (as it was for his predecessor, Al Capone) was that the Republican Party dominated the national level of government.

The Republicans have had scandals and corruption, but they tend to have less tolerant views than Democrats regarding the criminal actions of certain minorities: these minorities (Italian, Jewish, African-American, Latino) tend to be the ones who vote for Democrats. Under the Reagan Administration, the President's policies were so involved in dismantling the administrative structures set up since the New Deal (by Democrats) that he gave little real consideration to the Mob. This attitude was less apparent under his successor. George Bush made lawlessness a keystone of his 1988 Presidential Campaign, culminating in the unfair commercials showing one Willie Horton, an African-American released from a Massachusetts prison while Bush's opponent was Governor of that state, and who then committed another crime in Maryland. Bush had an extremely ruthless streak in him, one that stood comparison with Gotti's. As President, he seemed determined to nail Gotti once and for all.

In December 1990 the Federal Government arrested Gotti for murder and racketeering. The new trial demonstrated the full extent of demoralization within the Mafia. In the 1987 trial there was a distinct lack of willingness to testify against Gotti, based on fear; the murder of Willie Boy Johnson should have cemented this fear. But in 1990 another close Gotti associate, Sam 'the Bull' Gravano, willingly testified after his sister was shot by masked gunmen. Others too were soon singing. The ancient fears and loyalty of the system had been demolished by Gotti's own actions on the way up; he had only himself to blame.

Even so, the behaviour of the Federal Government in 'getting Gotti good' in this trial leaves an unpleasant feeling in many of us who despise the man. Barry Slotnick was not the defence counsel in this trial, but Gotti's normal legal expert, the brilliant and smooth Bruce Cutler. In the preliminary rounds of the Federal trial, Cutler made considerable inroads into the prosecution case by questioning the motives of witnesses like Gravano. Then, suddenly, the Federal Government stopped the trial to protest the continued appearance of Cutler as defence attorney. The prosecution had bugged Gotti's headquarters, and had tapes of him and Cutler talking about Mob business, so that it was argued that Cutler was potentially a defendant or witness himself. The court agreed, and Cutler was replaced by Albert Krieger. Krieger is a fine criminal lawyer too, but there is a tradition of a defendant having the lawyer of his or her choice, especially in a trial that may result in a long prison term. The action of the Gotti court, if it is accepted (and it looks as if it may be, as the Supreme Court of the United States is loaded with Republican appointees), is not a good precedent for the future. Curiously enough, after Gotti's trial ended on 3 April 1992, the Bush Administration made no effort either to prosecute Cutler or to use him as a witness. It seems that the Clinton Administration is not planning to prosecute him either.

The Teflon chipped that day in April 1992. Gotti was found guilty of five counts of murder and racketeering. He is now imprisoned for life, but his lawyers (Krieger, Cutler, and the civil-rights activist, William Kunstler) are appealing. One's reactions are distinctly mixed. The thought of such a 'good' neighbour and businessman back in society is sickening. But the thought of a government riding roughshod over any legal right (to show who really is 'Boss') may be worse.

Revised Versions

1

The A6 Case

BRYN EVANS

A CHANNEL 4 TELEVISION DOCUMENTARY in the summer of 1992 reawakened interest in the execution thirty years previously of James Hanratty for the shooting of Michael Gregsten. The incident at a lay-by on the A6, at that time the main road from London to the north-west of England, in the small hours of the morning of 23 August 1961, produced one of the most hotly disputed convictions of the twentieth century. The man hanged just over seven months later was a small-time burglar whom no one had ever seen with a gun, and who said he had never been within thirty miles of the murder scene. The police produced no one to contradict those statements apart from the murder victim's companion, who almost miraculously survived several bullets intended to kill her. She subsequently made one false identification of her assailant, and her second attempt was to have a fatal consequence.

The circumstances of the murder were bizarre. Gregsten, a married man in his mid-thirties, a research scientist, had been having an affair with Valerie Storie, a colleague in her early twenties, for several months. The family of Gregsten's wife had for some time been trying to put a stop to his adulterous relationship. On Tuesday, 22 August, as the light faded, the couple were sitting in the

front of Gregsten's grey Morris Minor in a lovers' lane
bisecting a cornfield in Buckinghamshire, about thirty
miles north of London.

Miss Storie later described how they were studying
maps for a forthcoming motor rally when there came
a tap at the window. Winding it down, Gregsten was
confronted by a man holding a revolver in his gloved
hand; his face could not be seen from the couple's
seated position. Saying: 'This is a hold-up. I am a
desperate man,' he climbed into the back of the car,
telling them not to turn round. From the man's arrival
at the car at about nine-thirty, there followed a strange
two hours. He told the couple that he was hungry –
that he had not eaten for two days – and that he
had been sleeping rough. He was, according to Storie,
immaculately dressed, which didn't square with his tale
of desperation. He kept saying, 'It's all right, there is
no hurry.' When people appeared at a house on the
edge of the field, he told Gregsten to drive to a further
corner of it.

At about eleven-thirty, he ordered Gregsten to drive
off, and directed him on a circuitous route around the
fringes of north-west London. After a couple of hours,
during which time Gregsten had been allowed out of
the car to purchase milk, and later cigarettes, the car
was heading up the A6 through Luton. The man in the
back said he wanted to 'kip', and told Gregsten to park
in a lay-by. The couple again pleaded with him to take
the car and make a getaway, but he asked Gregsten to
let him see a bag which was in the front of the car. As
the bag was being passed over, he shot Gregsten twice in
the head, killing him instantly. When Storie screamed,
'Why did you do that?' the man replied, 'He moved too
quick. I got frightened.'

After some minutes discussing with Storie whether
Gregsten was dead, he ordered her into the back of
the car, where he assaulted her. He then made her drag
Gregsten's body on to the lay-by. She sat down beside
it and begged the man to go. He said again that there

was no hurry, and told her to show him how the gears of the Morris worked. As he displayed more indecision, Storie produced a pound note and pleaded with him to take it and go. Having pocketed the note, he shot her from a distance of about six feet. She was badly injured, but pretended to be dead. After more indecision, he got into the car and drove off jerkily southwards, in the direction of London.

Storie was discovered about three and a half hours later by a farm labourer on his way to work. She was taken to hospital, paralysed from the waist down, as she was to remain, but she was able to give a description of the gunman which enabled the police to launch a man-hunt of almost unprecedented intensity; as the behaviour of the murderer over the nightmare five hours in the car was clearly unstable, proprietors of boarding-houses and small hotels were asked to report if any guests had been behaving oddly since Wednesday morning. Gregsten's car was found early on the Wednesday evening, badly parked in a road in Ilford, on the eastern outskirts of London; there were few forensic clues beyond a couple of bloodstains.

On the Sunday afternoon, the manager of a hotel in Finsbury Park, north London, was told by a guest that a man in the room next to hers had been there for days, pacing around and talking to himself. The manager informed the police, and the man was taken in for questioning. He had registered at the hotel on Wednesday under a false name. His real name was Peter Louis Alphon.

He would be thirty-one the next day; he worked part-time selling almanacs, and lived in a succession of cheap hotels. The police discovered that he had strange pseudo-religious and fascistic views, and apparently no friends. He had not seen his father for years, but he regularly met his mother, who lived near Streatham Common railway station in south London. She provided him with small amounts of money which he supplemented through odd jobs and a knowledge of greyhound racing, from which he profited through astute gambling. His alibi was that on the Tuesday evening he had visited his mother and then booked into a seedy hotel in Maida Vale in north-west London. This statement apparently satisfied the police.

On 7 September, fifteen days after the murder, a woman living in Richmond in Surrey who had placed a newspaper advertisement for a room to let was attacked by a man to whom she was showing the room, who screamed, 'I am the A6 killer,' before running out of the house. Four days later, spent cartridge cases from the murder weapon were discovered in a room in the same Maida Vale hotel where Alphon said he had spent the night of the murder. The gun itself had already been found, behind the back seat of a 36A London bus. The room in which the cartridge cases were found had been occupied on only one night in the three weeks since the murder, and then by an Indian man more than a week later. The night *before* the murder, however, the room had been occupied by a man called Ryan, giving a north London address. Alphon, who had told the police that he had stayed at the hotel the following night, the night of the murder itself, said that he had not been in Ryan's room. So the police had two men to investigate, Ryan and Alphon. Alphon's mother was interviewed and agreed that she had met her son on the night in question and given him a suitcase.

Over the following week, it was Alphon on whom the police came to concentrate. On 22 September, after Mrs Alphon, re-interviewed, had admitted that she had not seen her son for two months, the police launched a full-scale hunt for him, issuing a detailed description and going on television to appeal for help.

He walked into Scotland Yard late that night. The transcript of the interview, only made available in 1992, shows that he refused to say where the clothes were that he was wearing at the time of the murder. On 24 September he stood on an identity parade at Guy's Hospital before Valerie Storie, but she did not merely fail to pick him out but 'identified' one of the nine definitely innocent men in the line-up.

This failure to identify Alphon was absolutely crucial to the outcome of the case. He had stayed at the Maida Vale hotel. He had lied about part of his alibi. And he had been identified by the woman in Richmond as her assailant. But the case against him could not be made to 'stand up' without identification by Valerie Storie, the chief witness.

Having decided that they could not proceed against Alphon, the police focused their attention on the man named as Ryan in the Maida Vale hotel register. Until the case was closed, with the conviction some four and a half months later of that man, whose real name was James Hanratty, the police apparently could not be deflected from the idea that he was guilty as charged – although, as we have seen, one month after the murder they were as sure as they could be that they knew the guilty party, who was not Hanratty.

James Hanratty was a twenty-five-year-old petty criminal from Kingsbury in north London. He had spent much of the previous five years in prison for burglaries and thefts of and from motor cars. He bore little resemblance to Peter Alphon. He had not altered his behaviour since the murder, and indeed had broken into two houses in Stanmore in north-west London more than five weeks later. When he found out in the first week of October that the police were looking for him in connection with the A6 killing, he telephoned Scotland Yard to tell them he was not guilty – that he had been in Liverpool on the murder night, attempting to sell stolen jewellery through criminal contacts he had made while in prison. He was arrested in Blackpool on 11 October and taken to Bedford for an identity parade. Two out of four witnesses who said that they had seen Gregsten's car being driven after the murder picked out Hanratty as the driver. The next day, Valerie Storie identified Hanratty from a line-up on her ward in Stoke Mandeville Hospital, and he was charged with the murder.

Valerie Storie's identification of Hanratty probably decided his fate – but she had already identified someone demonstrably innocent in the line-up in which Peter Alphon stood. In interviews with police in hospital before both of those parades, she had expressed her fear of not being able to identify the man if confronted with him. This fact was only revealed in 1992, as was her statement within a few weeks of the murder that 'my memory of this man's face is fading'. But at Hanratty's trial, the leader of the investigation said: 'Her description of the murderer never changed from the day of the murder until now, and I have always regarded it as most reliable.' Whoever it was whom she identified on the first parade was never produced so that the jury could judge whether he resembled Hanratty. When she picked out Hanratty, his hair was a vivid tangerine colour because of having been badly dyed. The original description at the time of the crime, based on Miss Storie's word, was of a man with brown hair. Hanratty produced witnesses to say that in late August his hair had been dyed black.

Another factor which was to count against him was that the murderer had said, 'Call me Jim.' Prosecuting counsel told the jury that this implicated Hanratty – but papers produced for the first time in 1992 show Storie telling detectives long before Hanratty's arrest that 'Jim' was 'obviously not' the man's real name.

The finding of the spent cartridge cases in a hotel room known to have been used by Hanratty can only be explained in one of two ways. Either Hanratty had been careless enough to leave them there – or else someone planted them there to frame him. The fact that it was twenty days after Hanratty left the hotel before the cartridge cases turned up seems to support the latter explanation, but this possibility was not examined at his trial, simply because it never occurred to Hanratty or his lawyers that anyone had a reason to frame him.

What should have rendered all the evidence against Hanratty redundant was his alibi. He said that he had caught a train from London to Liverpool on the morning of Tuesday, 22 August, left a bag containing stolen jewellery in the left luggage office at Liverpool Lime Street railway station, and tried to find the fences he had met while recently at Liverpool's Walton Prison. He had not clearly remembered the name of the road where they lived, and at about 5.30 in the afternoon had enquired at a sweetshop staffed by an elderly woman and a young girl. Remarkably, an elderly woman was found who said she did remember a young man making such an enquiry. She had served in the sweetshop for only two days in the whole month of August, filling in for a holidaying relative. Those days were Monday the 21st and Tuesday the 22nd. At times on both those days, she had been helped by a young female relative. The police knew that Hanratty was in London all day on the Monday, staying at the Maida Vale hotel that night, so that Tuesday was the only possible day he could have made the enquiry. The police had to accept that if he was in a Liverpool sweetshop at half-past five, it was most unlikely that he was in a Buckinghamshire cornfield at half-past nine, because the train journey from Liverpool to London in those days took about four and a half hours.

However, what removed the credibility from Hanratty's alibi was the fact that after the trial had opened, he amended it. He still insisted that he had gone to Liverpool, left the bag, tried to find the fences, and gone into the sweetshop – but he now said that, being unable to find his criminal friends, he had caught a bus to the north Wales seaside resort of Rhyl, some thirty miles from Liverpool, where he had worked for a couple of days at a fairground about a month before. He had told the police that he had spent the night in Liverpool because he could not remember the address of the guesthouse in Rhyl where he had stayed and had never known the landlady's name. He had thought he would be able to bribe old criminal friends in Liverpool to say that he had been there that night, but none had obliged. He explained that, as he had arrived in the seaside town late on an evening during the holiday season, most of the guesthouses were full; after trying several, he was offered a bed in an attic bathroom – and therefore was not asked to sign the register and did not breakfast with the other guests.

Hanratty's amending of his alibi probably influenced the jury more than anything apart from Valerie Storie's identification of him. His presence in Rhyl at the time of the murder has since been corroborated by several people whom it was impossible to locate during and immediately after the trial because of the pressure of time.

If indeed he was not the murderer, then it certainly seems that the true culprit made a partially successful attempt to sound like him, and gave snippets of information to Gregsten and Storie which fitted Hanratty – although he also said and did things which were quite uncharacteristic of him. Afterwards, strong efforts were made to link Hanratty to the crime. What cannot be explained is how whoever decided on the partial impersonation and the planting of the cartridge cases in the hotel room could have known that Hanratty did not have a watertight alibi. The best guess is that the framer could not have known, and that the forged links to Hanratty were red herrings designed to distract the police. How it came about that both Hanratty and Alphon, the two prime suspects, stayed in the same hotel on successive nights remains a mystery.

There is, of course, another mystery: How did the strange goings-on in the car come about in the first place? What was the gunman's motive? It hardly seems likely to have been theft or rape, since the man took hours to get around to those offences, not to mention the murder and maiming. It may be that, as Alphon has claimed, the gunman was *employed* – that the motive was to break up the adulterous relationship, to get Gregsten to run off when he was told he could get out of the car to buy milk and cigarettes, in order to demonstrate to his mistress that he was not truly in love with her.

Whatever the truth of this, and whoever the gunman was, it is only logical to assume that he was *sent* to the cornfield, otherwise one has to believe that a deranged, immaculately dressed man was wandering around quiet country lanes with a gun, hatching wicked plans on the spur of the moment. The murder of Gregsten may have been an accident, as Alphon has claimed – an involuntary tightening of the trigger-finger under perceived threat – but the rape and subsequent shooting of Storie would then have to have been callous decisions to fabricate a sexual motive and to cover the murderer's tracks.

As you will know or will have gathered from things I have said, Peter Alphon has repeatedly confessed to the crime, most recently and in writing in 1992 – but whether he did or did not commit the crime has become almost a separate issue. To the question of whether James Hanratty was guilty, the answer has to be *almost certainly no*.

The edifice of facts in this case builds to the size and complexity of a crime novel, but the central point to keep in mind is this: the very presence of the man in the cornfield, his possession of a gun, his strange behaviour in the car, his sexual violence, his casual or psychopathic use of the gun, his inability to drive a perfectly ordinary car without instruction – not one of those factors coincides with James Hanratty's behaviour, traits or abilities. The bewildering speed of the case (Hanratty was dead less than six months after his arrest) has been replaced with the slower discovery of many new points, almost all of them in Hanratty's favour, over the last thirty years.

Within the Home Office, there are semen and blood samples from surviving members of Hanratty's family, finally proving or disproving whether it was he who was in the car that night. The Home Office has, however, resolutely refused to release the samples. The Channel Four documentary has revived public disquiet about the case, but there seems to be great insistence at the Home Office that Hanratty was guilty, and that

Alphon, with his tale of conspiracy, must at all costs be ignored.

2

Doubts About Hauptmann

THE LINDBERGH CASE HAS BEEN turned into a sort of fiction.

That has been achieved mainly through the efforts of certain authors of books about the case, makers of television programmes about it, writers of stage-plays said to be based upon it (a play of that kind was produced at an off-Broadway theatre in 1992), and a woman who for nearly sixty years has done her utmost to make people disbelieve the truths of the case. Early in 1993, the fiction was strengthened when, in an episode of a BBC television series, *Fame in the Twentieth Century*, the presenter, the Australian writer Clive James, told millions of viewers that the man executed for the kidnapping and murder of the Lindbergh baby 'was almost certainly innocent'.

Mr James's reference to the case was a postscript to comments on the immense fame of Colonel Charles A. Lindbergh, all because he had made the first solo aeroplane-flight across the Atlantic. That was in May 1927. Two years later, the 'secret' marriage of Lindbergh, the Lone Eagle, to Anne Morrow, a daughter of a rich politician, was given front-and-subsequent-pages coverage throughout the world. And so was the birth of their son, Charles Jr, in June 1930. Long before the arrival – the 'perfect landing' – of the 'Eaglet', Lindbergh had grown tired of being a public show. Seeking a refuge from fame, he bought a wooded estate a few miles from the small town of Hopewell, in the desolate Sourland region of New Jersey, and had a two-storeyed house built, to his precise specifications, in a clearing at the end of a long curving driveway from the road. Believing the publicity that he had come to despise, which made him out to be *everyone's* hero, and therefore inviolable, he did not consider the fact that so secluded a residence was ideally suited as the setting for a crime.

Apart from some finishing touches – including replacement of a shutter on one of the nursery windows, which had warped, making it impossible to fasten – the house was complete by March 1932. The Lindberghs had taken to spending long weekends there, the rest of the time at the Morrows' home at Englewood, fifty miles or so to the north-east, looking across the Hudson River to the Bronx, the northernmost borough of New York City. But that routine was broken on Tuesday, 1 March: as it was a miserable, blustery day, and the baby, now twenty months old, was suffering from a chill, Mrs Lindbergh decided to remain at the new house. Lindbergh, who spent part of the day in New York City, drove back in the evening, arriving at half-past eight; on his way through the servants' quarters, he paused to ask Betty Gow, the Scottish-born nanny, about his son's slight illness. The other servants, butler and cook, were a married couple, Oliver and Elsie Whateley, who were both from England.

At about ten past nine, soon after the Lindberghs finished dinner and went into the living room, they heard a noise – sounding to Lindbergh 'like the slats of an orange-box falling off a chair'. Supposing that the noise had come from the kitchen, they resumed the conversation that it had briefly interrupted.

At ten o'clock, Betty Gow went to the nursery to check that the baby was still sleeping as soundly as when she had left him two hours before, swaddled against the merest draught with a sleeping suit, a woollen shirt, and a sleeveless garment she had sewn together earlier in the evening with distinctive blue thread that she had got from Mrs Whateley: 'a proper little flannel shirt to put on next his skin.' Leaving the door open so as to give some light from the landing, she groped her way to the crib. The baby was not there. Betty Gow felt no alarm, for she assumed that Mrs Lindbergh, perhaps hearing the child crying, had taken him from the crib. She went to Mrs Lindbergh's room, found her on her own, and, fearful now, ran in search of Lindbergh, hoping against hope to see him holding his son – and, finding him in the library, alone, screamed to him to follow her back to the nursery. They searched the room, then every other part of the house, now with Mrs Lindbergh and the Whateleys helping – and then Lindbergh shouted to the butler to phone the police, grabbed a hunting rifle and ran through the front door, around the clearing and along the driveway to the road.

He had returned, had gone back to the nursery, before the first policemen arrived: the entire force of Hopewell, numbering two. He pointed to an open window, the one with the warped shutter, and to a white envelope on the muddied sill, saying that he had not touched it in case it bore the kidnapper's fingerprints. When the envelope was eventually opened, having been 'dusted' without result, it was found to contain a single sheet of white paper, also free of prints, on which a message was written in blue ink:

> Dear Sir
> Have 50000$ ready 25000$ in 20$ bills 15000 in 10$ bills and 10000 in 5$ bills. After 2–4 days we will inform you were [*sic*] to deliver the mony [*sic*] We warn you for making anyding [*sic*] public or for notify the police. The child is in gut [*sic*] care. Instruction [*or 'indication'*] for the letters are singnature

The 'singnature' was of two interlocking circles, with three holes near the perimeters.

Lindbergh and the local policemen went outside. Shining their torches on the muddy ground below the open window, they saw two indentations made by the ends of a ladder. The ladder itself was lying some twenty yards away. Obviously home-made, it was of three sections, each seven feet long. The two lower sections were connected (with dowel pins pressed through matching holes in the rails), and the top section, which the kidnapper had not needed so as to reach the window, was nearby. There were splits in the rails of the connected sections, almost certainly caused during the kidnapper's descent with a burden weighing thirty pounds, making a combined weight that overstrained the timber, particularly where the sections were held together with the dowel pins. Again almost certainly, the noise the Lindberghs had heard at about ten past nine was the splitting of the ladder-rails.

By midnight, the investigation was being carried out by officers of the New Jersey State Police, directly led by Colonel H. Norman Schwarzkopf, who had been in charge of the semi-military force since its formation eleven years before. (In the Gulf War of 1991, the Allied forces were commanded by his son, General Norman Schwarzkopf.) By daybreak, there were more state policemen at Hopewell than in the rest of New Jersey put together. Even so, they were outnumbered by reporters and cameramen, who were themselves outnumbered by sightseers. The early stages of the investigation, the most important ones, were a complete shambles. It has been said that Schwarzkopf and his aides 'suffered, under the sudden spotlight, from a bad attack of stage-fright,' but the truth of the matter is that the spotlight showed them up as incompetent detectives. None of them thought to measure, let alone make a plaster-cast, of a footprint, probably the kidnapper's, below the nursery window . . . the inspection of the nursery was superficial . . . dozens of people, not only policemen, were allowed to handle the ladder although it had not been thoroughly tested for fingerprints.

Three days after the crime, Lindbergh received, by post from Brooklyn, a second note from the kidnapper, repeating the warning against involving the police, saying that the baby was in 'gut health,' and raising the ransom demand to $70,000. The following day, another note, similar in tone, was delivered at the Manhattan office of Lindbergh's legal adviser. Lindbergh issued press statements to the effect that he was eager to negotiate, without bringing in the police. He also announced that, in case the kidnappers (plural, though there were several reasons, including the comparative modesty of the ransom demand, for believing that the crime was the work of an individual) did not wish to deal with him personally, he had authorized two New York bootleggers, Salvy Spitale and Irving Bitz, to act on his behalf. Among many other persons who offered their services as go-betweens were the presidents of Columbia and Princeton Universities; Al Capone, whose offer was contingent upon his being given leave of absence from the prison where he had recently begun serving an eleven-year sentence for tax-evasion – and John F. Condon, a retired school-teacher who had lived all of his seventy-two years in the Bronx, which he considered 'the most beautiful borough in the world'.

A week after the kidnapping, Condon's local news-paper, the *Home News*, printed a letter from him in which he pleaded with the kidnapper to communicate with him, promising both secrecy and the addition of a thousand dollars – 'all I can scrape together' – to the ransom money. Next day, he received a letter, containing a sealed enclosure, which said that if he was willing to act as go-between he should 'handel incloced letter personally' to Lindbergh and then remain at home every night. He phoned the Lindbergh house, read the letter to the person who answered, and, when told to open the enclosure, read that out as well: explicit instructions regarding the parcelling of the ransom money were followed by the circles-and-holes signature. Condon, asked to come to Hopewell, got a friend to drive him there. Comparison of the letter and the enclosure with the letters that had definitely been written by the kidnapper showed that the handwriting was much the same, there were similar errors of spelling and grammar, and the signatures matched. It was agreed that, in accordance with the kidnapper's instructions, a small ad should be placed in a New York paper, saying that the money was ready; the message would be signed 'Jafsie,' an acronym of Condon's initials.

Three nights later (Saturday, 12 March), a letter was delivered to Condon by a cab-driver who had received it, together with a dollar for the 'fare', from a man who had flagged him down a short distance away. Following the instructions in the letter, Condon went to a deserted 'frank-further stand', where he found a note directing him to Woodlawn Cemetery, in the Bronx. After wandering around there for some minutes, he was approached by a man who, speaking with a strong Germanic accent, said that he was one of a gang of five kidnappers, two of whom were women. Condon and the man, who called himself John, talked for over an hour, meanwhile moving from place to place in and near the cemetery. The man said that the baby was alive and well, receiving constant care aboard a boat. Just before he hurried off into the cover of woodland, he promised to send Condon 'a token' that would prove beyond doubt that he was not a hoaxer.

The token – the baby's sleeping suit, parcelled and sent by post – was delivered to Condon on 15 March. The negotiations continued, with Jafsie ads bringing replies through the post – till Saturday, 2 April, when final arrangements were made for payment of the ransom. The serial-numbers of the bills had been taken; at Condon's suggestion, the money was in two packets, one of $50,000, the original asking-price, and the other of $20,000. That night, Condon, in a car driven by Lindbergh, followed a trail of messages, at last to a dirt road beside St Raymond's Cemetery, where 'John' was waiting. Lindbergh heard him calling out to Condon to follow him into the cemetery. After some argument, the kidnapper agreed to accept the $50,000, and handed Condon a 'receipt' which, so he said, gave instructions for finding the baby. He ran off into the cemetery, and Condon returned to where Lindbergh was waiting. The note read:

> The boy is on the boad [*boat*] Nelly. It is a small boad 28 feet long. Two persons are on the boad. The [*they*] are innosent [*sic*]. You will find the boad between Horseneck Beach and Gay Head near Elizabeth Island.

Early next morning, Lindbergh began flying over that area, off the coast of Massachusetts. He continued the search till late on the following day, long after he had accepted that the 'boad Nelly' was a figment of the kidnapper's imagination.

On Thursday, 12 May, while Lindbergh was searching for another 'kidnap boat' (the invention of a man named John Hughes Curtis, whose motive for concocting a complicated hoax remains obscure), the decomposed body of a baby boy was found, quite by chance, lying face-down in a thicket beside a little-used road five miles from the Lindbergh home. Any slight doubt as to whether the body was that of the kidnapped child was dispelled by Lindbergh, who, returning in response to a radio-message, viewed the body in a mortuary and recognized several physical characteristics, particularly a malformation of the bones in one foot; also by Betty Gow, who identified garments, one of which was the flannel shirt which she had stitched together with unusual blue thread. According to the local coroner, the principal cause of death was 'fractured skull due to external violence.'

At last released from constraints imposed by the possibility that the baby was still alive, law officers, not only of New Jersey, set about tracing the man who had committed the double crime against 'the first family of America'. Not that there was much to go on. The best hope seemed to be that the criminal would be caught through his spending of the ransom money. The list of the serial-numbers was circulated to banks, and cashiers were given an incentive to watch out for the bills by the offer of a reward of seven dollars, partly contributed by Lindbergh, for the spotting of any of them. They soon started to appear, usually in deposits made by shops, cafes and filling stations; depositors were interviewed in the hope that they could connect the particular bills with specific transactions and recall something about the customer. As each bill, or batch of bills, was spotted, the location of the place where it had turned up was marked on a map, which soon showed a preponderance of transactions in the Bronx and the contiguous northern part of Manhattan.

Part of the ransom money was in gold notes, and in May 1933, following President Roosevelt's order that all such notes were to be exchanged for ordinary currency at a Federal Reserve Bank, someone signing himself J. J. Faulkner exchanged nearly three thousand dollars' worth of them at the bank in New York City; soon after it was noticed that they came from the ransom (they constituted the largest transaction ever spotted), it was found that no one named Faulkner lived at the address given by the exchanger, whom the cashier could not describe at all.

Later in the year, the police sought help from attendants at filling stations, saying that whenever a customer paid with a bill of ten or twenty dollars, the attendant should write the licence-number of the customer's vehicle on the bill. That initiative would produce the vital break in the case.

While the 'Lindbergh squads' of detectives doggedly stuck at their respective tasks – each squad acting virtually independently, and some of them as if in competition rather than cooperation with the others – a most unconventional detective was at work.

His name was Arthur Koehler. He was a 'wood technologist' of the Forest Service of the Department of Agriculture. Shortly after the kidnap case became one of murder as well, he began trying to establish where the criminal had bought the timber to construct the ladder.

178

Having identified the types of timber, he concentrated on that which was of North Carolina pine. Microscopic examination showed marks made by a particular kind of mechanical plane; the records of manufacturers of such machines revealed that twenty-five were in use; most of those were ruled out because they were used only to dress other types of timber. After months of searching, Koehler found the plane he was looking for at a mill in South Carolina; because a non-standard pulley had been installed in the autumn of 1931, the machine made additional marks that were uniquely the same as those on some of the ladder rails. Koehler visited all of the timber companies to which the mill had shipped 'ladder-size' boards of North Carolina pine during the five months between the pulley-changing and the kidnapping. Only at one of the yards – that of the National Lumber & Millwork Co, in the Bronx – did he find a remnant on which there was an 'extraordinary mark', resulting from the temporary nicking of one of the frequently-sharpened blades of the mechanical plane, that he had detected in his examination of the ladder. He was sure that he had found the yard at which most of the timber for the ladder had been bought. Not quite all of it: four apparently old nail-holes at one end of the rail he designated as No. 16, as well as the fact that the rail was grubbier than the rest, indicated that the timber was secondhand, that it had been used for some other purpose before becoming part of the ladder; the most likely explanation for the presence of Rail 16 was that the kidnapper, finding that he had not bought quite enough timber, had made up the deficit with an old piece that happened to be nearby. Koehler, whose achievements had set him among the greatest forensic investigators, could do no more – for the time being, that is.

On Tuesday, 18 September 1934, more than two and a half years after the kidnapping, a cashier at a branch of the Corn Exchange Bank in the Bronx spotted a ten-dollar ransom bill in a deposit from the Warner-Quinlan Co, a local filling station. A vehicle licence-number – 4U-13-14-NY – was written on the margin of the bill. The filling-station manager and his assistant said that the bill had come from a customer driving a blue 1930 Dodge saloon, who had bought five gallons of petrol, costing just under a dollar. The Licence Bureau provided the name and address of the owner of the car: Bruno Richard Hauptmann, 1279 East 222nd Street, the Bronx. The registration card showed that he was almost thirty-five, of medium build, with blue eyes and 'muddy blond' hair, German-born, and a carpenter by trade.

Further inquiries revealed that he was an illegal immigrant (and it was subsequently learned that he had served a five-year prison sentence in Germany for burglaries and a highway robbery – in which he had threatened to kill two women wheeling prams – and that he was wanted by the German police, who considered him 'exceptionally sly and clever,' because in 1923 he had escaped from custody while awaiting trial for other burglaries, and fled to America). In 1925, he had married Anna Schoeffler, a waitress, also German-born, who in November 1933 had given birth to a son, named Manfred in homage to Baron Manfred von Richthoven, the German air-ace of the Great War.

At nine o'clock on the morning of the 19th, Hauptmann was arrested after he had backed his car out of the garage in the yard of his house and started driving towards Manhattan. He was searched before being taken to a police station, and a twenty-dollar ransom bill was found folded in his wallet.

Much more of the ransom money – $14,600 of it – was found in various hiding-places, including holes burrowed through a block of wood, in his garage. Faintly scribbled in pencil on the inside of a closet-door in the house were John F. Condon's phone number and address; also what appeared to be the serial numbers of banknotes – none corresponding with that of any of the ransom bills.

According to Hauptmann, the ransom money had come into his possession in December 1933 – though without his knowledge at that time. He had, he said, agreed to look after a shoe-box for a friend and business associate, Isidor Fisch, who was about to take a trip to Germany. Fisch had died during the trip. Hauptmann said that he had forgotten about the box till the summer of 1934, when rain-water had seeped into the closet where he had stowed it; the box, damaged by the water, had been further damaged, to the extent that the contents were revealed, when he had accidentally hit it with a broom. Without saying a word to his wife, he had hidden the bills in the garage. As Fisch had died owing him money, he had felt justified in dipping into the small fortune, unaware that it was criminal loot.

Hauptmann had worked regularly as a carpenter till 2 April 1932, the day when the ransom was paid, but had done only a few odd jobs since; his wife had given up her job as a waitress in December 1932. Their joint earnings since April 1932 amounted to just over a thousand dollars. And yet during that time, though Hauptmann had meanwhile bought several luxury items, gone on hunting trips, and paid for his wife to visit her relatives in Germany, his capital had risen from just under five thousand dollars to just over forty thousand – including the money in the garage. He attributed his recent affluence to successful dealings in the stock market, but examination of his brokerage accounts showed that he had made a total loss of nearly six thousand dollars. Many of his bank deposits in the same period consisted largely or wholly of coins (two deposits of about four hundred dollars were made up entirely of silver), which suggested to the investigators that he had systematically 'laundered' ransom bills by using them for small purchases and getting lots of change. There was nothing to indicate that Isidor Fisch, a small-time dealer in cheap furs, was better off after April 1932 than previously: he had continued to get by without a car, had remained in the cheapest of digs, had borrowed money and tried to borrow more – and apparently would not have been able to afford the trip to Germany from which he did not return if Hauptmann had not stepped in at the last minute with a loan of $2,000.

When Hauptmann was interviewed by the District Attorney of the Bronx (with a shorthand-writer taking down the questions and answers), he was shown the detached closet-door and asked: 'Your handwriting is on it?' 'Yes, all over it,' he replied. He said that he could not make out some of the notations and could not explain some of the others. Why had he made a note of Condon's address? 'I must have read it in the paper about the story. I was a little bit interest, and keep a little bit record of it, and maybe I was just on the closet and was reading the paper and put down the address . . . It is possible that a shelf or two shelves in the closet, and after a while I put new papers always on the closet, and we just got the paper where this case was in and I followed the story, of course, and I put the address on there . . . I can't give you any explanation about the [*Condon's*] telephone number.' (At a subsequent interview, he said that he was in the habit of jotting down notes of important events on walls in the house.) He said that the serial numbers on the closet-door were of large bills that Fisch had given him to buy shares.

Handwriting experts compared the kidnapper's writing (on the demands to Lindbergh and on the ransom-arranging letters to Condon) with specimens of Hauptmann's writing before his arrest. In the summer of 1932, detailed analysis of the notes had proved that, as was to be expected, the writing was disguised; but the analysis had picked up many repeated letters and words that the kidnapper had failed to disguise – also a number of misspellings and peculiar locutions. Since the analysis, one of the experts had examined the writing of more than three hundred men questioned by the police, without finding a single specimen with sufficient resemblances to the notes. The kidnapper/Hauptmann comparisons left the experts in no doubt that no one but Hauptmann could have written the notes. Their conviction was based not only upon matching formations but also upon Hauptmann's writing of a dictated 'test paragraph' containing words that the kidnapper had misspelt – for instance, 'anything' and 'something' as 'anyding' and 'someding', 'our' as 'ouer', 'were' as 'where', 'later' as 'latter'. Hauptmann misspelt every one of the 'trick words' in exactly the way the kidnapper had.

Almost a year before, Arthur Koehler had suggested to the police that they should interview every customer of the National Lumber & Millwork Co. in the months preceding the crime; the suggestion had not been followed up. But by the time that Koehler was summoned to Hauptmann's house, a few blocks from the timber yard, a checking of the company's records had shown that Hauptmann had bought ten dollars' worth of timber there at the very end of 1931. Hauptmann either could not or would not say what he had used the purchase for. Koehler inspected the woodwork in and of the house – lastly, that in and of the attic. There, he immediately noticed that part of one of the flooring boards was missing; that it had been sawn off was evident from the fact that sawdust clung to the lathes at the end of the truncated board. He compared Rail 16, the odd one out, with the board. Not only were the two pieces of the same type of wood, and the same lateral dimensions, but the graining and the annual rings corresponded. And when an end of Rail 16 was placed near the end of the board, the four nail-holes in the rail matched exactly four nail-holes in the joist below; two of the holes in the rail had been driven in diagonally, at the selfsame respective angles as the matching holes in the joist. With the holes aligned, there was a two-inch gap between the rail and the board, indicating to Koehler that the maker of the ladder, having sawn off rather more than he needed, had sawn the rail to the required length. Seeking further evidence that Hauptmann had made the ladder, Koehler examined the contents of the carpenter's chest in the garage-cum-workshop, paying particular attention to the planes, the blades of which he examined under a microscope, scrutinizing them for nicks and other imperfections. He used the planes on blocks of 'neutral wood', and found that one of them left ridges that coincided exactly with the ridges he had observed in hand-planed surfaces of a side of the ladder and all of its rungs; the matching of the ridges, as unique to a particular plane-blade as fingerprints are to a particular hand, was apparent to the naked eye. Proving that the plane was Hauptmann's, a bracket in the garage bore the same ridges.

At identification parades, Hauptmann was picked out by various eye-witnesses – and, though not on a parade, by an ear-witness, Lindbergh, who said that Hauptmann's voice was that of the man he had heard calling out to Condon at St Raymond's Cemetery on the night when the ransom was handed over. Condon was both an eye- and an ear-witness, saying that Hauptmann was definitely the 'Cemetery John' with whom he had negotiated on two occasions, for nearly two hours in all. Among others who claimed to recognize Hauptmann were the cab-driver to whom the criminal had given a letter for delivery to Condon; a woman who said that, during the 'Jafsie period', she had seen Hauptmann watching Condon at a Bronx railway station; a box-office girl at a Manhattan cinema, who said that he was the man who in November 1933 had paid for a ticket with a ransom bill; and two men living near Hopewell – one an illiterate hillbilly with an unsavoury reputation, the other an octogenarian whose eyesight had deteriorated – who said that they had seen Hauptmann near the Lindbergh estate shortly before the kidnapping. Condon was the only one of the eye/ear-witnesses whose evidence was stronger than doubtful.

The trial of Hauptmann began on the second day of 1935 in the pretty courthouse in the small town of Flemington, New Jersey, which was jam-packed throughout the trial with journalists (including Damon Runyon, Walter Winchell and Ford Maddox Ford),

184

press photographers and movie cameramen, and sight-seers (including show-business personalities, such as Jack Benny and Clifton Webb, and members of high society, some accompanied by their publicity agents). The prosecution was led by David T. Wilentz, the pugnacious Attorney-General of New Jersey (he died, aged ninety-three, in 1988); the defence by Edward J. Reilly, 'the Bull of Brooklyn', who had been briefed in more than two thousand murder trials and whose fee in the Hauptmann case was partly paid by a newspaper in return for 'exclusives' from the defendant and his wife. The trial dawdled on till 13 February, when the jury of eight men and four women, all local people, each now famous wherever newspapers were circulated, having deliberated for just over eleven hours, returned a verdict of Guilty of Murder in the First Degree, without recommendation of life imprisonment.

There were, of course, any number of appeals, each postponing the execution. Meanwhile, Anna Hauptmann went on a fund-raising tour of places with large populations of German-Americans, and told audiences at Hauptmann-is-Innocent rallies what they wanted to hear: that her husband was the victim of a frame-up, chosen as such simply because he was German. Near the end of 1935 (shortly before the Lindberghs, wanting to get away from it all, sailed for England with their second son Jon, intending to settle here), Harold G. Hoffman, the Governor of New Jersey, who happened to be planning a bid to become the Republican candidate for the Presidency, got himself on to front pages and into editorials by saying that he had visited Hauptmann in his cell and that he had grave doubts as to whether the case had been solved. Hoffman kept himself in the news for the next couple of months – by declaring his faith in Hauptmann's Fisch story and pooh-poohing Koehler's findings, by announcing that he had hired private detectives to re-examine the case, by talking of 'new evidence' (which turned out to be worthless, either because it was immaterial or because it was proved to have been fabricated), and, in January 1936, by granting Hauptmann a thirty-day stay of execution – during which a vainglorious detective named Ellis Parker, a friend of Hoffman's, entered the case. A few days before Hauptmann was again scheduled to die, Parker and his son produced a detailed 'confession' signed by Paul Wendel, a disbarred lawyer – but refused to produce Wendel until Attorney-General Wilentz insisted on knowing where he could be found: in a mental institution, where he had been confined for some weeks on Parker Senior's orders. The execution, re-scheduled to take place on the last day of March, was postponed while a grand jury pored over Wendel's 'confession' and discussed his account of how he had been kidnapped by a gang, kept in a cellar in Brooklyn, where he had been tortured till he was ready to sign anything, and then taken to the mental institution.

On Friday, 3 April 1936, shortly after the grand jury voted to drop the Wendel case, Hauptmann, still protesting his innocence, was executed in the electric chair at Trenton Prison.

That necessarily brief account does not, of course, include every bit of the long story. But I don't think I have left out any points of real importance. If I have, the omissions are unintended, not meant to mislead. I shall, in a minute, refer to points that another writer has suggested are important but which, in fact, are not. If my account contains any inaccuracies, they must be of a trivial nature. I have not amended truths to suit a purpose.

Bruno Richard Hauptmann was guilty of the kidnapping and murder of the Lindbergh baby.
I state that, not as an opinion, but as a fact.

Harold G. Hoffman and Ellis Peters were not the first persons, nor (as I intimated when I began) the last, to try to muddy the truths of the case. For a discussion of some of the quaint theory-books published before 1985, I can do no better than quote Patterson Smith, the leading American bookdealer specializing in factual crime material:

Although it is now not often realized, the Lindbergh kidnapping attracted sceptics from the start. Just after the story broke in 1932, Laura Vitray, a Hearst reporter, rushed into print with a little-known book, *The Great Lindbergh Hullabaloo: An Unorthodox Account*. Unorthodox it is.

Vitray, sensing a hoax, wrote derisively of the Lindbergh family, referring to the child as 'the golden-haired Eaglet', and accusing certain vaguely defined 'powers' of having 'deliberately arranged the Lindbergh "kidnapping", not for ransom, but as a story, to divert public attention from the grave disaster that threatens this nation at their own hands today.'

Laura Vitray had a sister sceptic in Mary Belle Spencer, a Chicago lawyer who seems to have had an animus against the massive law-enforcement effort that was thrown into the hunt for the Lindbergh child and its kidnapper. In 1933, after the discovery of the child's body but before the arrest of Hauptmann, she published a pamphlet bearing the cover title, *No. 2310, Criminal File: Exposed! Aviator's Baby Was Never Kidnapped or Murdered*.

Her argument was that no crime had been shown to have been committed, the infant being perfectly capable of having wandered off on its own to meet its death by animals in the woods. She presents the text of a mock trial in which she defends a vagrant 'John Doe' who has been indicted for kidnap and murder. In her burlesque, she makes thinly veiled substitutions for names prominent in the case, such as 'Limberg' for Lindbergh and 'Elizabeth Gah' for Betty Gow. (For reasons unknown to me, on the front cover she has covered the original line of type, which read 'Limberg's Baby', with a correction strip reading 'Aviator's Baby'.)

This curious work, which is now rare, almost had severe consequences for the trial of Hauptmann. Prior to the proceedings, copies were mailed to the panel of jurymen, causing the judge to consider granting a change in venue.

H. L. Mencken said that the Lindbergh case was 'the biggest story since the Resurrection'. Concerning Hauptmann's guilt there seemed to be little doubt, for he was tied to the crime by a web of circumstantial evidence which, taken as a whole, was so strong that it seemed that no one possessed of reason could challenge the certainty of his guilt.

But a challenge did come. Anthony Scaduto, in *Scapegoat* (1976), marshalled some 500 pages of evidence and argument in an attempt to demonstrate that Hauptmann, at most guilty of extortion, ended his life the victim of a judicial murder by the state. Scaduto's arguments, given additional publicity by Hauptmann's widow, seeking vindication for her husband, attracted much attention and gained many adherents.

An issue is raised here on which I wish to ruminate. In a quarter-century of dealing in material on criminal justice history, I have had contact with many writers and researchers seeking material for new books on past crimes. Often a product of such endeavours will be the first of its kind on a given crime; often it will be a retelling, with added information or a new analysis, of a familiar crime narrative; often it will add to the literature yet another theory in explanation of a crime never satisfactorily explained.

On rare occasions, of which *Scapegoat* is one, it will offer a radically divergent theory of a crime hitherto considered settled. Of all crime books published, those posing revisionist theories tend to attract the greatest media attention. They are 'news'. Far from merely adding to our knowledge of a past event or re-embellishing a tale previously grown stale in the telling, they say to us, 'You've been wrong about

188

this case.' And if someone is thought to have been unjustly convicted and executed, the news value is all the stronger.

It has, after all, been observed that Americans have a greater sense of injustice than of justice. When a revisionist account reaches reviewers, the arguments put forward by its author can seem extraordinarily compelling, for very often the book does not aim for balance but selects only those facts that support its divergent thesis.

Moreover – and this is very important – the reviewer of a book on crime written for the general public often has little or no background in the case which could help him weigh the author's novel contentions against countervailing evidence. The reviewer sees only one side of the story, and it usually looks good.

If you infer from these musings that I do not accept Anthony Scaduto's thesis about Hauptmann's innocence, you are correct.

Another quote, this one from the brilliant American lawyer Louis Nizer, who, having coined the term 'analytical syndrome', explains:

It is possible to take the record of any trial and by minute dissection and post-facto reasoning demonstrate that witnesses for either side made egregious errors or lied. Then, by ascribing critical weight to the exposed facts, the conclusion is reached that the verdict was fraudulently obtained. This was the process by which the Warren Commission Report [on the assassination of President Kennedy] was challenged in a spate of books. To cite just one illustration, a constable deputy sheriff described the rifle which had been found on the sixth floor of the Book Depository Building, Dallas, as a Mauser, instead of a Mannlicher-Carcano, which it was. Out of this innocent error, due to ignorance or excitement, sprouted the theory that the real assassin's rifle

189

had been spirited away and Lee Harvey Oswald's rifle planted on the scene to involve him. Multiply this incident by many others, such as someone's testimony that shots were heard coming from the mall, and the 'hiding' of the death X-rays of the President (since revealed), and you have a gigantic conspiracy by foreign agents, or government officials, or New Orleans homosexuals, or lord knows what, to fix the blame on an innocent man, Oswald. Of course, all this was nonsense, and subsequent events have confirmed the accuracy of the Report.

The analytical syndrome can be used to discredit any verdict, from the commonest automobile negligence case to the most involved anti-trust or proxy contest.

Anthony Scaduto uses the analytical syndrome. And so does Ludovic Kennedy, the British television personality who in 1985 published a 438-page book, *The Airman and the Carpenter: The Lindbergh Case and the Framing of Richard Hauptmann*, which must have convinced many, perhaps most, of its readers that Hauptmann was the victim of a miscarriage of justice.

Since Kennedy's is the most recent Hauptmann-was-innocent book, and since he repeats the Scaduto notions that he likes best, I shall concentrate on his view of the case.

First, though, let me quote his explanation of what invariably persuades him to produce so-and-so-was-innocent books and of what his 'method of investigation' is. My interpolations may, at this stage, seem to be nit-picking, but I promise you that they are pertinent. Kennedy: 'I have been asked whether in cases I have investigated I have ever been convinced of the complainant's guilt. The answer is no, because I have never pursued cases where I have been uncertain about guilt or innocence.' (The words 'guilt or' are redundant, for Kennedy has only pursued cases where his initial instinct assured him that the persons found guilty were innocent.) 'In those cases I have written about, my initial instincts that the person in question was not guilty have been fully confirmed by subsequent investigations.' ('Fully confirmed'? To his own satisfaction, he must mean.) 'It should however be emphasized that, contrary to popular belief, cases of guilty men proclaiming their innocence and *continuing to do so with evidence to back it up* are so rare as to be almost non-existent.' (Heaven knows what that means. One assumes that the backing-up evidence refers to the proclamations rather than the innocence of the guilty men. Perhaps not: as I shall demonstrate, Kennedy, following the general example set by Humpty Dumpty, does tend to use the word evidence rather loosely – as a description of things that may have happened, things that are rumoured to have happened, and things that certainly didn't happen. In any event, how does Kennedy know that his statement is true, considering that he has never investigated any such cases?) Speaking of his 'method of investigation,' Kennedy says: 'My starting-point has always been a presumption of innocence, and in all my cases I have found a narrative story based on that presumption to be far more convincing than a continued assumption of guilt.'

Using the Kennedy Method (which is far more complicated than he has just made it out to be), one would have no difficulty in 'proving', say, that Adolf Hitler was pro-semitic – or, having plumped for a presumption of guilt, that St Francis of Assisi was a vivisectionist. Actually – *confirming* popular belief – the annals of crime are strewn with undoubtedly guilty persons, many of them users of the analytical syndrome, who never wavered from pleading innocence.

Here is one of Kennedy's several versions, all much the same, of how he came to the conclusion that Hauptmann was innocent:

'The place was my hotel bedroom, the time around 8 a.m. [on a day in 1981]. As one often does in New York at that time of day, I was flicking idly through the television channels while awaiting the arrival of orange juice and coffee. I did not even know which channel I was tuned to when there swam into my vision a very old lady proclaiming with vehemence that her husband was innocent of the crime of which he had been convicted. I sat up and paid attention for this was, as it were, my territory . . . Slowly it dawned on me – for the scene had been set before I had tuned in – that the old lady was none other than Anna Hauptmann, the widow of Richard Hauptmann . . . And then I remembered from Eton days a picture that would be seared on my mind for ever, a full-page photograph of the haunted unshaven face of Richard Hauptmann as it first appeared after his arrest and then again, on the day of his electrocution two years later.

'And now, nearly half a century on, here was his widow not only proclaiming his innocence but telling Tom Brokaw (and this was the peg for the interview) that as a result of new information about the case, she was taking out a suit against the State of New Jersey for her husband's wrongful conviction and execution . . . I felt the old adrenalin surging through me and a sense of heady exhilaration; for I thought it improbable in the extreme that an old lady in her eighties would have agreed, forty-four years after her husband's death, to have travelled all the way to New York to appear on an early morning television show to assert her husband's innocence and launch a suit against a powerful state if she knew (and she would have known) that her husband was guilty; not unless she was out of her mind, and she did not seem to me to be that.'

Let us examine Kennedy's criteria for an 'extreme improbability':

1 *That 'an old lady in her eighties would have agreed . . . to have travelled all the way to New York to appear on an early morning television show . . .'* The old lady in her eighties (as opposed to a young lady in her eighties, who really would deserve sympathy) was as fit as a flea. Near the end of Kennedy's book, more than four hundred pages away from his account of Mrs Hauptmann's appearance on television, he reveals that, four years later, she was 'still amazingly active and mentally alert'. Her journey 'all the way to New York' sounds a very long way indeed; but, in fact, she had only come from Philadelphia (which is a shorter distance from Hopewell than Hopewell is from New York); all her expenses were paid, all arrangements made, by the television company, who no doubt also paid her an appearance fee. With no disrespect to her, it is reasonable to think that she would have been glad to put herself out far more than she did in order to appear on a popular television chatter show, doing her utmost to sway public opinion in favour of her claim that her husband had been 'Wrongfully, Corruptly, and Unjustly' executed – and, incidentally, that she was entitled to damages of a hundred million dollars.

2 *That unless Mrs Hauptmann was out of her mind (and she seemed perfectly sane to the perfectly sane Kennedy), she would not have gone to such trouble 'if she knew (and she would have known) that her husband was guilty'.* Excluding Kennedy, Scaduto & Co. (and Mrs Hauptmann's lawyer, who was presumably working on a contingency-fee basis that he would receive a percentage of any profits from the legal action), it is impossible to think of any campaigning pro-Hauptmannite whose utterances on the case should be taken with more salt than those of Mrs Hauptmann. Following her husband's arrest, she too was grilled; her questioners were unable to break her story that her husband had told her nothing of the ransom money hidden at first in the house and then in the garage, she had never chanced on any of it, and she had accepted his explanations as to how he, though hardly ever working, was able to pay the domestic bills, buy luxury items, and send her off to Germany for a three months' holiday. Supposing her story was true, then there is no doubt whatsoever that Hauptmann, if he was the kidnapper, never told her that he was, and never gave her the least reason for suspecting that he was. Therefore (and quite apart from the fact that it would be most unexpected

193

if she, a determinedly trusting and loving wife, no less determinedly trusting as a widow, were ever to speak of any suspicion of Hauptmann that may have crossed her mind against her will), all that she can say first-hand in defence of her husband is that, until his arrest, she had no reason for thinking that he was connected in any way with any crimes committed in the spring of 1932. The best one can say of that is that it is negative evidence – about as useful as the evidence of an eye-witness who claims that he didn't witness anything. A proverb seems apropos, not only of Mrs Hauptmann but also of her confederates: 'There are none so blind as those that will not see.'

In every complex criminal case, the evidence for the prosecution can be divided into two sorts: *salient* and *secondary*. If the salient evidence stays intact, no amount of doubt concerning any, even all, of the secondary evidence has the slightest weakening effect upon the strength of the salient evidence – which, in the case of Hauptmann, was this:

1) He had spent some of the ransom money and was in possession of a large part of the remainder, which he had hidden away in his garage, some of it in specially carpentered hidy-holes. 2) He was the writer of the ransom notes. 3) Part of the ladder, specially carpentered for the kidnapping, had been sawn from the floor of carpenter Hauptmann's attic. 4) He had written John F. Condon's address and telephone number on the inside of a closet-door in his home. 5) He had given up full-time work on the very day that the ransom was paid.

Let us look at the first four points one by one – leaving out the last, which was and is undisputed.

1) Hauptmann's explanation for his possession of the ransom money was that a shoe-box had been left with him by Isidor Fisch, who had since died, and that, after Fisch's death, he, Hauptmann, who meanwhile had given no thought to the box, let alone been at

194

all curious as to what it contained, had opened it and found a small fortune, which – without thinking twice, and without saying a word to his poor, hard-working wife – he had treated as a windfall (but one which, though it never occurred to him that he might be handling 'hot money,' he felt that he needed to stash away in various hiding-places, some of which he used his long-unused carpentry tools to create).

There isn't a scrap of evidence that supports Hauptmann's Fisch story. But Kennedy does his best – or rather, worst – to lead readers up a garden path to a belief that the story was corroborated. Some of those readers will have been taken in. One of Kennedy's methods is to state something with complete assurance, in the hope that readers will assume that they must have missed his earlier proving of the statement or forgotten it, and will therefore accept his statement as gospel. His first more than slight reference to Isidor Fisch appears on page 134, and is given particular emphasis because it is at the start of a sub-chapter: 'Of all the diverse characters who people the Lindbergh kidnapping story, the most mysterious, the most enigmatic, the most sinister is undoubtedly Isidor Fisch.' It is safe to say that Kennedy would feel that he had been treated disgracefully, unfairly, improperly, if the author of an article about him began by saying: 'Of all the diverse characters who have written about the Lindbergh kidnapping case, the most mysterious, the most enigmatic, the most sinister, is undoubtedly Ludovic Kennedy' – and that he would be still more upset if the author, continuing, failed (as, of course, he would) to substantiate the statement. Yet Kennedy doesn't seem to care that he fails to substantiate his statement about the dead Fisch.

The most Kennedy is able *to pretend* to prove in his efforts to bolster the Fisch story concerns Hauptmann's best friend, Hans Kloppenburg. On page 243, he says: 'A key witness in the matter was Hans Kloppenburg, who had seen Fisch arrive at Hauptmann's home with the shoe-box, hand it to Hauptmann, and the two of them go into the kitchen with it.' A few of those readers who have frail memories, and most of those with a healthy suspicion of anything that Kennedy says as if stating a fact, will thumb back a hundred pages to the account of the 'handing over the shoe-box' incident: 'on December 2 [1933], the Hauptmanns gave a farewell party for Fisch [who was sailing to Germany on the 6th] . . . When Fisch came he brought a package wrapped in paper and tied with string which Kloppenburg, who was standing by the door, described as a shoe-box.' Kennedy then says – but without explaining that he is now quoting, would you believe, from *Hauptmann's* story – that 'Fisch asked if Hauptmann would look after the package while he was away . . . and Hauptmann readily agreed.'

So: between Kennedy's two accounts, a package wrapped in paper and tied with string, and described by Kloppenburg as a shoe-box, becomes '*the* [my italics] shoe-box' – and the package, only carried by Fisch in the first account, is handed over to Hauptmann in the second. Perhaps Kloppenburg did describe the package as a shoe-box when interviewed by Kennedy or his researcher half a century after his fleeting glimpse of it; but at the trial, answering a question from his best friend's counsel, he described it only as a package, and gave a rough idea of its dimensions – which made it as likely to have been a boxed strudel, Fisch's contribution to the party fare, as a shoe-box filled with ransom money. Under cross-examination, Kloppenburg admitted that he 'did not remember seeing Fisch leave the Hauptmann home on the night of the farewell party, and therefore could not say whether Fisch took the package away with him.' Imagine what Kennedy would have made of it if Kloppenburg had testified that Fisch left empty-handed: he could have turned that into 'clinching evidence' that the shoe-box story was true – as easily as anyone disagreeing with

196

him, and willing to swallow the shame attached to resorting to a similarly fallacious way of arguing, might use the empty-handedness to turn the strudel possibility into the strudel 'fact'.

2) Whoever kidnapped the Lindbergh baby also tricked the $50,000 from John F. Condon. There is conclusive proof of that in the fact that all of the ransom notes, including the one left in the nursery, bore the overlapping-circles 'singnature'; if anyone like Kennedy insists upon having incontrovertible corroboration of that conclusive proof, there is the fact that the baby's sleeping suit was mailed to Condon by the ransomer. Kennedy may, without thinking, protest that there is a possibility that more than one person took part in the kidnapping – that the person who left the note in the nursery was not the writer of that note or the subsequent ones. All right – but I doubt if he, inventive as he is, can conjure that point around to make an ersatz semblance of help for his argument that Hauptmann was neither *a* kidnapper nor *the* ransomer – just a poor, framed illegal immigrant who, having been given a small fortune to look after, decided, as any sensible person would, to keep it for himself.

At Hauptmann's trial, the prosecution called eight handwriting examiners, all of whom were convinced that the ransom notes had been written by the defendant. Before those examiners gave evidence, the defence had half a dozen examiners prepared to say the opposite; but by the time the latter were needed, all but one had dropped out, some admitting that they had done so because they had completely changed their minds. The defence touted around for replacements, but, unable to entice a single one, were left with the only steadfast member of the original half-dozen – and had difficulty in persuading the judge that he, John Trendley of East St Louis, was qualified to give evidence as an expert witness.

One doesn't need to be a handwriting examiner to *know*, from looking at the hundreds of word and letter comparisons presented at the trial, that Hauptmann wrote the ransom notes. The resemblances between words and letters in the notes and words and letters in documents written by Hauptmann cannot be explained away; a few of the comparisons appear on pages 199 and 200. And, as if further proof were needed, words and letters in a 'farewell declaration of innocence' that Hauptmann sent to Governor Hoffman demonstrate his guilt.

What does Kennedy make of this? Not a lot. Though he includes J. Vreeland Haring's classic and massive book, *The Hand of Hauptmann*, which is packed with illustrations of the comparisons, among what he claims are the 'Sources' of *his* book, he makes no obvious use of its contents. Despite the fact that he includes 75 half-tone and line illustrations in his book, not one is of a handwriting comparison – which surely means that he was unable to find a single comparison which he thought doubtful enough for him to pooh-pooh. What does he say about the prosecution's handwriting examiners? Not a lot. Inter alia, this: that they looked 'like senior members of an old folks' bowling club'. (In fact, only one of the eight was older at the time of the trial than Kennedy was when he published his book.) What does he say about the handwriting evidence? Not a lot – indeed, even less. This: 'As the combined testimonies [of the handwriting examiners for the prosecution] run to some five hundred pages of the trial transcript and are much concerned with technicalities – the shape of a "t" or the curl of a "y" – and as their conclusions were later challenged by the defence's lone expert using the same material, it is not proposed to go into these in any detail.' *Five hundred pages* of evidence against Hauptmann, and he does not propose to go into it in any detail! – a) because much of it is technical (as much expert evidence at most trials is – does he mean, then, that all such technical expert evidence can be disregarded by jurors?) and b) because the defence had a 'lone

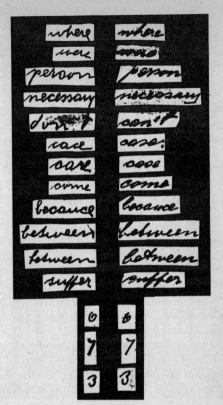

Kidnapper's handwriting on left, Hauptmann's on right

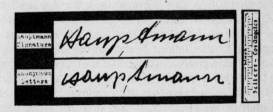

Top: Hauptmann's normal signature.
Bottom: A 'signature' composed of letters cut from the ransom notes.

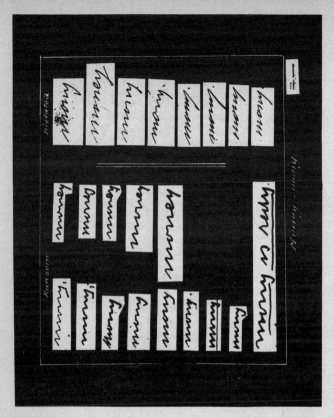

expert' so reckless or desperate for a fee that, having glanced through fifty documents in the space of two and a half hours (under cross-examination, Trendley was forced to admit that that was the extent of his prep), he was willing to be a minority of one.

So far as Kennedy would like us to be concerned, the fact that Hauptmann's handwriting was the same as that of the ransom notes is irrelevant to the question of whether or not Hauptmann was the ransomer. Forget about that, he says hopefully – let's concentrate on the all-important matter that words misspelt in the ransom notes were similarly misspelt by Hauptmann

200

in his 'request writings'. Those similarities, every single one of the many of them, are easily explained away (he says): speaking of all investigators, he says: 'When contradictory evidence appears, they ignore it, unwilling to admit that their original belief was false; and the longer the original belief is held, the more difficult it becomes to shift. When no corroborative evidence appears to reinforce the belief, it has to be manufactured . . .' Ergo: the investigators who got the request writings from Hauptmann forced him to misspell certain words in the same way that those words were misspelt in the ransom notes. Isn't that obvious? Well, it might be – but what about the fact that many of the misspelt words appear in the same misspelt way in documents written by Hauptmann before his arrest? I doubt if you will be surprised to learn that Kennedy tries to gloss over the obvious answer to that question. Rather surprisingly, he does not seek to reincarnate a notion that the defence had at the start of the trial, but dropped once it was established that Hauptmann and Fisch were not introduced till after the kidnapping: the notion was that Fisch had, for some reason or other, forged Hauptmann's writing on the ransom notes. One last point about those notes: proof that they were not written by Fisch is as undoubtable as the proof that they were written by Hauptmann.

3) Even if only in terms of persistence, Arthur Koehler's work in tracking the kidnap ladder to the man who made it is among the most admirable pieces of detection of all time. There is not a scrap of evidence to suggest that Koehler (who completed the leg-work part of his investigation nearly a year before anyone had any reason to suspect Hauptmann) was not entirely honest. The same can be said of Koehler's helper, Lewis Bornmann, of the New Jersey State Police. Kennedy, irritated by such honesty, sneers at 'these two jokers'. On the same page as that sneer (221), he *states* that Koehler's discovery that

ladder-rail No. 16 was from the floor of Hauptmann's attic is completely discredited by the fact that he did not instantly 'proclaim it [the discovery] to the world'. On the same page as the sneer and the statement, he speaks of a defence 'trump card' (in fact, a trumped-up card: it was some non-evidence of an alibi, which I shall refer to shortly) – and does not consider that it is at all devalued by the fact that the defence kept it up their sleeve for months. Heads, he wins – tails, honest investigators lose.

He is forced to use the chestnut ploy of asking the reader to be as reasonable-minded as he is: Is it likely that a sensible person (Hauptmann) would do a silly thing (cut timber from his attic for a kidnap-ladder rail)? Since almost all sensible criminals who are arrested are found out because they have done silly things, if all defence counsel used the ploy with invariable success, almost all sensible criminals would be acquitted. That might please Kennedy but I would venture to suggest that all other sensible law-abiding persons would take a dim view of it. The fact that Hauptmann made the ladder from different sources is no more strange than the fact that, rather than finding or making one hiding place for his 'windfall', he found or made more than one.

Kennedy, incidentally, accepts Hauptmann's description of the ladder as 'ramshackle' – meaning that it must have been made by someone without carpentering skills. Kennedy has seen the ladder. So have I. Even if I spent months trying to, I certainly couldn't make as good a job. Could Kennedy? If he says yes, and has a few months to spare, would he mind putting his manual mastery where his mouth is? If he likes, he can appoint a non-carpenter proxy. Is that a fair challenge?

As part of Governor Hoffman's re-examination of the case, a so-called wood expert visited the attic – and told Hoffman that he could prove that Rail 16 had not come from there, saying that his conclusion was partly based on the fact that when nails were pressed through the holes in the rail and into the holes in the joist, they protruded a quarter of an inch. Koehler was summoned to the house, and it was discovered that, since his last visit, quarter-inch wooden plugs had been pushed into the holes in the joist. Kennedy ascribes the post-trial jiggery-pokery in the attic to an act of nature – or rather, he accepts without question Hoffman's subsequent comment that an unidentified someone had told him that the plugs were just 'fibrous fragments' that, in the abnormal course of dead-wooden events, had sort of congealed together to look the spitting image of plugs. Still relying on Hoffman, he quotes him as saying (in 1936): 'I have in my possession a photograph of the ladder made the day after the commission of the crime. It is a clear photograph, in which the knots and grains are distinctly shown, and Rail 16 can be easily identified; but neither in the original nor in a copy magnified ten times can the alleged nail-holes be found.' Has anyone ever seen the photograph or the enlargement? Has Kennedy? Had Hoffman? The four nail-holes are clearly visible in police photographs among those taken of the ladder on 8 March 1932. It is all very well for Kennedy to admit (well away from the Hoffman quote) that Hoffman was posthumously proved to have embezzled $300,000 from the State he governed – and almost as well to comment that Hoffman's crookedness 'in no way diminishes the courageous stand he took in championing the cause of Hauptmann's innocence . . .' – but it is reasonable to assume that if anyone who contributed to the verdict at Hauptmann's trial had afterwards turned out to be crooked, even only slightly so compared with Hoffman, Kennedy would have used that fact as a reason for disbelieving any anti-Hauptmann evidence from that contributor. Come to think of it, one doesn't need to assume: Kennedy, in seeking to discredit the eye-witness evidence of the Hopewell hillbilly I mentioned on page 184 (whose evidence *was*, surely everyone agrees, dubious), reports that, a couple of months after the trial, the hillbilly was 'clapped into jail for stealing a road grader and selling it for $50.'

Kennedy doesn't seem to have understood all of Koehler's evidence. For instance, there are times when he speaks of Rail 16 when what he is really talking about is the board in the attic from which, according to Koehler, Rail 16 was cut. In his account of the quizzing of Koehler in the attic on 26 March 1936, he says that Hoffman's 'wood expert', Arch Loney (can anyone doubt that Loney was the plug-ugly?), 'pointed out that Rail 16 [the board] was a sixteenth of an inch thicker than the other boards, but Koehler didn't have an answer to that'. The statement that Koehler was stumped is untrue. Having already answered questions from Loney that showed that the latter's knowledge of carpentry was rudimentary, Koehler patiently explained that 'as the attic was unfinished, uneven flooring was to be expected.' After a couple more questions from Loney, and immediate answers from Koehler, an observer said to Attorney-General Wilentz, speaking loudly enough for everyone to hear: 'I can't believe that Koehler has been brought all the way from Wisconsin for this!' That exclamation seems to have prompted Hoffman – not Loney, you notice – to demonstrate that nails pushed through the holes in Rail 16 and into the holes in the joist did not go all the way down (because, as was proved later in the day, plugs had mysteriously become inserted in the holes in the joist).

4) During the week after Hauptmann's arrest, he twice, on separate occasions, neither of them a third-degree session, admitted that he had written John F. Condon's address and telephone number on the inside of a closet-door in his home. At the trial, when cross-examined about the writing, he got into a hopeless tangle in trying to explain away his original explanation. One can understand why. Clearly, when

Hauptmann was first asked about the writing – shown it – he, flustered because he *knew* that the writing was his and *believed* that the writing was undoubtedly identifiable as his, felt that there was no point in lying that he had not made the notations, and gave the only explanation for them that he could invent: that he was in the habit of jotting down references to important events on doors (a habit of which there was no other sign in the house).

Kennedy, who gets angry about hearsay that doesn't suit his purpose, is only too happy to accept hearsay that does. On page 204 he says, no ifs or buts, that a *Daily News* reporter, Tom Cassidy, 'planted' the writing 'as a joke . . . either late on September 24 [1934] or on the morning of the 25th . . . He then smudged the writing as though an attempt had been made to wipe it out.' Well, that's sure enough, isn't it? Isn't it? Well, no – because it turns out that 'Cassidy's joke' is something that in the late 1970s was rumoured to have been rumoured towards the end of 1934: rumoured both times, what's more, by reporters – the 1934 ones among those who, so Kennedy says four pages later, 'went overboard completely, not hesitating to print all sorts of allegations and rumours as fact.' Not satisfied with the little that the reporter-rumourers of the 1970s had to say, Kennedy adds a rumour of his own, that 'Cassidy got word to the Bronx police' – presumably so as to make his joke hilarious. According to all three of the 1970s rumourers, Cassidy was too pleased with his joke to worry that, if he had really perpetrated it, he could be imprisoned: 'Hell, he bragged about it all over town' . . . 'He admitted it to me and Ellis Parker, he told everybody about it' . . . 'He told a bunch of us . . .' Like most rumourers, these protested too much: if the joke was such common knowledge, how is it that the defence lawyers were never let in on it? Kennedy doesn't explain that (not even when, exactly a hundred pages later, he speaks of a moment during the trial 'after Wilentz had been questioning

Hauptmann about *Tom Cassidy's writing* [my italics] on the inside trim of the closet').

Perhaps he believes that Hauptmann's leading counsel, Edward J. Reilly, did hear about the joke, and decided that it must not be mentioned, for fear that it might help to get his client acquitted. Kennedy, you see, suspects that Reilly was actually a mole-type extra counsel for the prosecution. If ever a statement deserved to be followed by several exclamation marks, that one does. Kennedy's suspicion is based on two things, one being the fact that part of Reilly's fee had been guaranteed by 'the anti-Hauptmann Hearst Press' (in return for exclusives from Hauptmann and his wife), the other being Kennedy's feeling that Reilly did not ask all the questions he should have asked. If Kennedy knew anything about the art, which it is, of cross-examination, he would know that the reason for virtually all of the Reilly unquestions which he cites is covered by a maxim of cross-examination: Never ask a question if you don't already know the answer.

It is surprising if he has never heard that maxim, for he himself, as an 'investigator', pays great regard to a variation on it: Never ask a question if there is the slightest risk of getting an answer that does not accord with your preconception.

Twenty pages after 'proving' that Tom Cassidy was a psychopathic joker, Kennedy reinstates Cassidy as an upright citizen, his word even better than his bond, the last person in the world one would suspect of fabricating evidence. The reinstatement is in aid of 'proving' that Hauptmann did a full day's work at the Majestic Apartments, Manhattan, on 1 March 1932, in the evening of which the Lindbergh baby was kidnapped. Cassidy, so Kennedy says, unearthed payroll records showing that Hauptmann worked at the Majestic Apartments till 5 p.m. (A few Kennedy sentences later, '5 p.m.' becomes '5 or 6 p.m.') Finding Kennedy's Majestic argument incomprehensible, even after umpteen attempts to fathom it, I gave photostats of the pages to four friends – a barrister, a coroner, a forensic scientist, a book-publisher's editor – and was relieved to hear from all four that they too were baffled. The trouble, I think, is that Kennedy, for once believing that he has a lot of evidence that needs no help from him, presents all of it – so much that one cannot see the wood for the trees.

But supposing that the Majestic argument is valid, the documentary evidence for it untampered with by pro-Hauptmann researchers, it certainly doesn't mean that Hauptmann had a sort of alibi. Kennedy is guessing again when he says, on page 173: 'The police realized that if he [Hauptmann] was working at the Majestic Apartments until five or six [*sic*] on Tuesday, March 1, it was unlikely that he was putting a ladder up against the nursery window at Hopewell three or four hours later . . .' Let us allow Kennedy his unsubstantiated assumption that Hauptmann worked an hour of overtime, from five till six. Even if Hauptmann had driven the sixty miles from the Bronx to Hopewell at the dangerously slow average speed of 20 m.p.h., he would have arrived at the Lindberghs' house with ample time to spare before the kidnapping, at about ten minutes past nine. Not that he would have *wanted* ample time: the longer he loitered near the house, the more danger there was that he or his parked car would be observed.

Kennedy, as well as saying that Hauptmann almost had an alibi for the time of the kidnapping, says that Hauptmann had a complete alibi for the night of Saturday, 2 April, when Condon handed over the ransom money to 'Cemetery John': 'It being the first Saturday of the month, Hauptmann and Hans Kloppenburg had their regular musical get-together.' At the trial, under direct examination, Kloppenburg testified that he 'recalled being at the Hauptmann home on the night of 2 April 1932, it being a custom to gather for an evening on the first Saturday of each month'. (Kloppenburg's helpfulness to Hauptmann is rather hard to reconcile with the tale he told half a century after the trial, which

207

was that he had first been grilled by detectives – 'They were trying to scare me with the electric chair so that I wouldn't testify' – and then by David Wilentz: 'A day or so later, I think it was the day before I testified, there was a story in the newspapers that police were about to arrest a second man in the kidnapping. That was me they were talking about. They were trying to scare me so I would shut up. And I *was* scared.') Under cross-examination, Kloppenburg 'admitted telling the Bronx District Attorney, shortly after Hauptmann was arrested, that he could not remember when he saw Hauptmann in March or April 1932, because "that is too long ago".' Under redirect examination, he gave two further reasons for remembering the date of the evening of music: 'There was some sort of April Fool joke' and 'Mrs Hauptmann spoke of wanting to go and see her niece the following day.' (Did anyone else, even Tom Cassidy, play April Fool jokes after April Fools' Day? So far as anyone seems to know, Mrs Hauptmann may have paid frequent Sunday visits to her niece – or frequently, on Saturdays and other days, spoken of wanting to see her niece.) Under re-cross-examination, Kloppenburg admitted that he had 'talked with Detective Sergeant Wallace, of the New York City Police, shortly before Christmas, 1934, and at that time said he could not recall any dates upon which he saw Hauptmann in March or April 1932'. Can anyone be as certain as Kennedy claims to be that the Hauptmanns and their best friend Hans were musically trio-ed when, in a cemetery not far away, the ransom was paid?

Four years after the publication of his book on the Lindbergh case, Kennedy published his memoirs, *On My Way to the Club* (Collins, London, 1989). Meanwhile, in 1987, a book by Jim Fisher, *The Lindbergh Case*, was published by Rutgers University Press (New Brunswick and London). Kennedy makes a chapter of his memoirs from how he came to the conclusion that Hauptmann was innocent; what he considers most important of the things he subsequently found so as to give ostensible support to his conclusion. And he then, in the space of a page, launches an hysterical attack on Fisher – all because, so he says, Fisher doesn't pay enough attention to 'information . . . used by Mrs Hauptmann's lawyer, Tony Scaduto and myself'. It is the most despicable page of writing that I have come across in a very long while.

I hold no brief for Fisher – whom I have never met, and who has written me just one letter, that in reply to a single letter I wrote to him – other than that his book is honest, any errors in it that I have noticed being slight and unintended. Which is more than can be said for some books.

I shall not comment on those parts of Kennedy's attack on Fisher which are gratuitous, entirely irrelevant to the Lindbergh case – for I could only do so after repeating them. They should never have been published. Since Kennedy also makes a snide remark about Rutgers University Press, I shall express my surprise that *his* publishers, known to be reputable, permitted him to say such things.

Kennedy states: 'so concerned were the New Jersey authorities by Mrs Hauptmann's suits and the books by Tony Scaduto and myself that they gave their backing to . . . *The Lindbergh Case*.' That is untrue.

Kennedy states: 'the police officer in charge of the Lindbergh room at [the New Jersey] police headquarters became consultant to [Fisher's] project.' That is also untrue. Fisher received no more help from the policeman-curator than Kennedy would have been offered if he had requested help. (Incidentally, the untrue statement is pretty rich, coming from Kennedy – who employed Anthony Scaduto's wife as his researcher.)

Near the foot of the page, Kennedy says that, round about the time when Fisher's book was published, he was 'disappointed to hear that a [television] treatment based on my book and submitted to all three American networks had been turned down. Professionally, I was told, they all thought it a fascinating story that would make a gripping screenplay, but as network producers they did not feel they could support a programme whose conclusions were contrary to those arrived at by the American courts, and not yet reversed by them. The New Jersey establishment had triumphed again!!' Of all the many ridiculous comments made by Kennedy, that one takes the biscuit. Before writing his book, he cobbled interviews with pro-Hauptmannites into a television programme, *Who Killed the Lindbergh Baby?*, which was shown in Britain and America; soon afterwards, a television movie based on the case, starring Anthony Hopkins as poor Bruno, was shown in both countries; in 1989, Mrs Hauptmann and her lawyer, with other pro-Hauptmannites, appeared in a documentary that was shown throughout America. Currently, one of the three American networks is preparing a documentary (which, so I understand, will exhume the potty notion that the body identified as that of the Lindbergh baby was that of another murdered infant – that Charles Lindbergh Jr, having been reared by foster-parents who accepted him from the kidnapper, is still alive, one of half a dozen men in their sixties who claim to be him, entitled to a share of the Lindbergh fortune).

Right to the end of *The Airman and the Carpenter*, Kennedy omits facts that don't appeal to him. Apart from slight mentions in passing, none value-judgemental, all that he says about either Paul Wendel's retracted confession or Ellis Parker is this: '[During the weekend before the execution,] there had been a new and extraordinary development in this most extraordinary of cases in that all members of the New Jersey Court of Pardons had received a twenty-five-page confession to the Lindbergh baby kidnapping and murder by a fifty-year-old disbarred Trenton attorney and convicted perjuror (who was also wanted for fraud) by the name of Paul Wendel. This was not as crazy a confession as at first thought, since it had been made to none other than Ellis Parker, Hoffman's friend and the chief of Burlington County detectives [earlier described by Kennedy as a 'brilliant investigator']. Ellis was instructed to deliver

Wendel to Mercer County detectives who took him before a Justice of the Peace to be arraigned for murder before being lodged in the Mercer County Jail. Once there he immediately repudiated the confession, claiming that he had been kidnapped by Ellis Parker and his son Ellis Junior, taken to a mental hospital for a number of days, tortured there and forced to sign the confession under duress. It seemed to many that this, if true, was a last desperate effort by Parker, convinced that Hauptmann was innocent, to save him from the chair.' That, so far as Kennedy is concerned, is, importantly, all. Any reader of his book who has not read other books on the case must be left thinking that Wendel may have committed the crimes for which Hauptmann was executed.

The continuation of the Wendel/Parker story (which Kennedy, if he had felt like it, could have recounted in his last chapter, which deals with those post-execution events which he did feel like recounting) is as follows:

Wendel's account of his being abducted and tortured into making a false confession was investigated by the District Attorney of Brooklyn and proved true. Four of the gang of six confessed; one of the four died before the trial, but the others were sentenced to twenty years' imprisonment in Sing Sing. As Governor Hoffman refused to extradite the two ring-leaders, Ellis Parker and his son, to Brooklyn, Wendel got the United States Attorney-General to agree that the charges were the concern of New Jersey's federal grand jury, which handed down an indictment charging the Parkers with conspiracy under the Lindbergh Law (the statute, enacted in 1932, which made the kidnapping and transportation of a person across state lines punishable by imprisonment for life). Ellis Parker was sentenced to six years' imprisonment, his son to three, in a federal penitentiary. (And so the only law enforcement officer influentially involved in the Lindbergh case whom Kennedy does not accuse of crookedness, and the only one he has a nice – 'brilliant' – word to say about, was the only one proved to be a crook.) By using appeal procedures much as Hauptmann had done, the Parkers managed to remain at large till the summer of 1939, when they were imprisoned at Lewisburg, Pennsylvania. Early in the following year, Ellis Parker died of a brain tumour in the prison hospital; his son was released a few months later.

There is a saying that 'no one suddenly becomes a murderer.' More likely to be true, it seems to me, is a saying that I have just invented: 'No writer on criminal cases suddenly becomes an unreliable writer.' It would be valuable to crime historians, and others, if someone with the time and the research resources were to examine the 'miscarriage-of-justice books' published by Kennedy before he published *The Airman and the Carpenter*. Let me be absolutely clear: I don't know much about any of the cases covered, and so have no particular grounds for wondering if any of those books may have helped towards the miscarriage of justice that a guilty man was prematurely freed from imprisonment and/or pardoned and/or given compensation.

I applaud an idea mooted in the January 1988 edition of the journal of the American Academy of Forensic Sciences as a direct reaction to *The Airman and the Carpenter*:

> There are positive steps that the Academy can take to educate the reviewing press and the public when a book such as *The Airman and the Carpenter* presents the document or other scientific evidence in an unfair or biased manner. Each section of the Academy would appoint a book-review editor charged with reviewing those chapters of new books dealing with his particular discipline. If he found the information to be fairly presented, nothing further would be required. However, should the information prove to be deceptive, inaccurate, or incomplete, the reviewer would contact the major newspapers and magazines with his critique of the

offending portion. This would seem to be one of the ways a forensic science group can fight back against the misinformation disseminated in books like *The Airman and the Carpenter*.